YORKSHIRE DIALECT

John Waddington-Feather

Published by Feather Books
PO Box 438
Shrewsbury SY3 0WN, UK
Tele/fax; 01743 872177

Website URL: http://www.waddysweb.freeuk.com
e-mail: john@jjwfeather.co.uk

© John Waddington-Feather 1970, 1980, 2002, 2010

First published 1970 by Dalesman Publishing Company.
Second edition 1977
Reprinted 1980, 2002

This edition published by Feather Books 2010

Cover image *Langstrothdale*

ISBN: 1 84175 107 3

Contents

Part One: Page

A History of Yorkshire Dialect Celtic Place-Names 5

Dialects of the Old English Period (500-1150) 8

Dialects of the Middle English Period (1150-1450) 17

Modern English and Yorkshire Dialects (1450-present) . . 21

Part Two:

A History of and Selections
      from Yorkshire Dialect Literature 27

Books for Further Reading. 99

The author acknowledges the assistance he has received from the Yorkshire Dialect Society in collecting material for this book, and also the kind permission to reproduce their works given by writers connected with the Dialect Society.

Introduction

SINCE the first edition of "Yorkshire Dialect" in 1970, there has been a continued growth in the interest and study of English dialects. Perhaps the need of people to relate to local cultures and language in a world which continually tries to standardise us and make us more and more uniform is one factor that has made people look at their native dialects again. Perhaps it is simply that the richness of English dialects has been overlooked for so long. Whatever the reason, it is true that more research has gone into English dialects since 1945 than at any other time, and has brought to a wider public a deeper understanding of the rich folk-speech and writing peculiar to regional English.

In this respect, it is worthwhile recording the lifetime efforts of the late Professor Harold Orton and Dr. Wilfrid J. Halliday, who both contributed immeasurably to dialect scholarship; Orton through his linguistic research, and Halliday, not only as a linguistic scholar, but also as a Yorkshire dialect writer and critic. Halliday's editorial work, I believe, has not received the acclaim it deserves, nor has late Stanley Ellis, another lifelong researcher of dialects, who has done much to promote interest in and understanding of them. To these three scholars I respectfully dedicate this edition of "Yorkshire Dialect".

in northern latitudes about 400 AD, combined to give them the incentive to migrate. The rich settlements of the Celts in Britain, guarded by Roman troops, had been attacked on piratical raids long before the Romans eventually left. Roman watchtowers along the east coast of Yorkshire and further south bear testimony to the menace these Germanic pirates were.

When the Romans withdrew, rivalry among Celtic leaders and attacks by Pictish tribes from Scotland quickly reduced the country to a chaotic state. Vortigern, a Celtic leader in Kent, called in two Jutish warriors, Hengist and Horsa, to defend his territory from attack. Word quickly spread that Britain was undefended and a massive invasion of these islands by the Germanic tribes then took place.

The Jutes, as well as settling in Kent, colonised parts of Surrey, Hampshire and the Isle of Wight. Various Saxon tribes took possession of the rest of the south and west, giving their names to the present counties of Middlesex (middle Saxons), Essex (east Saxons) and Sussex (south Saxons). The old kingdom of Wessex is also still perpetuated in the novels of Thomas Hardy and administrative bodies in the west. The Anglian tribes settled in the Midlands and northern England. The east Angles are still remembered in the regional name East Anglia. The whole country, too, became named after them—England, the land of the Angles, just as Britain had been named after the last Celtic people to invade, the Brythronic tribes.

The language of the Germanic invaders was probably already split into dialects before they settled in England during the 5th and 6th centuries. Certainly by about 600 AD the country was split up into four very marked dialect speech areas. There were the Saxon dialects of the south and west, the Kentish dialects of the south-east, and two sorts of Anglian dialect: Northumbrian, the speech of the tribes who had gone north of the Humber, and Mercian, the speech of the Midland Angles. Yorkshire in 600 AD spoke entirely Northumbrian dialect, though later, as we shall see, the dialect of the Midlands made incursions into south and west Yorkshire.

In 600 AD the area which comprises modern Yorkshire was split up into three kingdoms, under the overlordship of the greater kingdom of Northumbria. The three kingdoms were the two Anglian kingdoms of Deira, covering what was roughly the East Riding and much of the North Riding, and Bernicia, extending northwards to the Scottish border and westwards to Cumberland. Then there was the Celtic kingdom of Elmete, still independent with few if any Anglian settlements in it. Elmete covered roughly the area contained by the present West Riding and it was governed by the British king Certic just before its Anglian conquest.

Politically, and probably numerically at first, the Celts in Elmete were strong enough to retain their identity until well into the early Anglo-Saxon period. In 616 AD, however, Edwin, King of Northumbria, occupied Elmete and expelled Certic as an act of revenge for the murder of one of Edwin's relatives when Edwin and he had been exiled by an earlier Northumbrian king and had sought refuge in Elmete. The previous year, 615 AD, the Northumbrians had also defeated a British army at Chester, and after the invasion of Elmete by Edwin in 616 an alliance was made between Cadwallon, King of Wales, and the Midland Anglian king, Penda, the pagan King of Mercia. They attacked Edwin and slew him at the Battle of Hatfield, near Doncaster. In 632 AD, Penda took over Edwin's lands in Yorkshire.

Penda's sovereignty over the West Riding lasted for more than 20 years until his own death in battle at Winwaed (probably Winn Moor near Leeds) in 655 AD. Incidentally this battle is also important because the pagan Penda's lands were taken over by his victor Oswi, Edwin's nephew, who was a Christian, and Christianity became the national religion, bringing with it the spread of education through its monasteries and priories.

During this period Mercian influence made itself felt in several ways in the West Riding. It came at the beginning of a period of Anglian colonisation in the old Celtic kingdom. Since Northumbrian settlement had been taking place only since 600 AD, a matter of 16 years, Northumbrian influence at this stage was not very strong. Possibly, too, the native Celtic population would be more sympathetic to Penda, being allied to Cadwallon. So perhaps, Mercian settlers would feel more inclined to settle in the former British kingdom than they would in the hostile Northumbrian territory to the east and north.

The place-names of the West Riding well illustrate the process of its colonisation, and they may give us a clue to the start of a process which has made the West Riding dialect so different from the dialects of the North and East Ridings. If we take the pronunciation of the word "sheep" as an example of the differences between Mercian dialect and Northumbrian dialect, we see that the Northumbrian word is "scip" (pronounced like "skeep") and the Mercian word is "seep" (pronounced like "shep" with a long vowel sound). Where the Northumbrian Angles settled there are place-names derived from "scip," such as Shipley, Shibden and, later, Skipton. Yet where the Mercian Angles settled there are place-names meaning the same thing but spelt differently to agree with their old pronunciation. Examples of Mercian settlement are Shepley, near Huddersfield, and Sheepscar in Leeds. Shepton Mallet in Somerset has the same Mercian spelling.

Another typical Midland word which occurs almost entirely in the south of the Riding, an area of great Mercian colonisation, is the word "worth," meaning an enclosure. This word in placenames is very common south of the Wharfe and links this region with North Midland county placenames such as Lutterworth and Tamworth. Around Keighley there is a cluster of these placenames such as Haworth, Oakworth, Hainworth, Cullingworth and Ryshworth. Elsewhere in south Yorkshire there are places like Illingworth, Wadsworth, Wentworth and Hemsworth.

Other place-name links with the Mercians are words such as "royd," a clearing, found in place and personal names such as Holroyd and Ackroyd; and "pightel," an enclosure, in placenames such as Pickles and Pighills. Yet another link with Mercian occupation during the 7th century is "bury" denoting a fortified place and found in present Midland place-names like Banbury and Wednesbury. The Northumbrian word was "borough," which the Norsemen who came later also used. The River Aire seems to be the boundary between the Mercian "bury" form (which is found in Dewsbury, Almondbury and Stanbury) and the Northumbrian "borough" form (in Knaresborough, Boroughbridge and Scarborough). Airedale in general seems to be the northern limit of early Mercian settlement, though dialect development characteristic of the Midlands carried this boundary further north in succeeding centuries.

Yorkshire dialect, like the Standard Language, has changed considerably over the centuries since it was first introduced. To begin with, there was no standard form of English to influence it. Between 500 AD and about 1100 AD there were four main English dialect areas and these have continued to develop to the present day. A Standard Language evolved only in the 15th century when economic and cultural influences made it necessary for a standard language to be used in the main centres of commerce and industry, especially London, when French ceased to be the language of the merchant and ruling classes.

The dialects spoken by Penda and Edwin were much more complicated than their modern counterparts spoken in Yorkshire and the Midlands. The Northumbrian and Mercian dialects were inflected like modern German. They changed the ends of their words to make meaning out of sentences rather than putting their words into a fixed order as we do today. Like some modern European languages, such as French and German, the nouns in Mercian and Northumbrian dialects had genders. They were masculine and feminine or neuter. They had five cases, which showed whether the noun was doing action or receiving it; and there were many other complicated differences in structure which made these early dialects quite different from their modern equivalents and modern Standard English.

Vestiges of them remain in current Yorkshire dialects and the pronunciation of these early dialect words are still recognisable in some present dialect words. Old English plural endings such as "childer," "een" and "shoon" still exist in Yorkshire dialects when they have been replaced in the standard tongue by "children," "eyes" and "shoes." The Northumbrian word "hus," for house, is still used in east and north Yorkshire dialects, and in some areas mother and father are still pronounced in a similar way to their Anglian pronunciation of "moder" and "fader." When the West Riding man talks about "samming summat off t'grahnd" he is using a word derived directly from the Old English verb "samian," meaning to collect, to gather together, which has disappeared altogether from the standard language.

All these Yorkshire dialect words and terms come from the speech of the first Germanic invaders of the 5th and 6th centuries, but in the 9th century a further invasion took place which enriched the dialect vocabulary tremendously, especially in the East and North Ridings. Northumbria was invaded by a Danish army in 865 AD. Yorkshire was part of a Viking empire until the Norman-French established their rule over the country over two centuries later. It was an invasion which destroyed a flourishing literary culture in Northumbria, at that time a leading seat of scholarship in Europe. Henceforth, English learning and culture were developed in the southern English kingdom of Wessex ruled by King Alfred. Winchester and Exeter, not York or Durham, Lindisfarne or Ripon, became the centres of great English scholarship, for the monasteries and abbeys that had fostered the golden age of learning in Northumbria were destroyed by the invading Danish troops.

The Danish army went on a long campaign throughout England using Yorkshire as a supply base, and in 876 AD part of the marauding force settled under Halfdene, their leader, in Yorkshire. He divided up the lands of the Northumbrians among his troops, who started colonising and farming tracts of previously uncultivated land. A Danish capital was established at Jorvik, now York. The Danes mainly preferred the flat arable land in the East Riding, leaving the difficult terrain of the West Riding Pennines and the North Riding Moors to the Anglians and Norsemen.

Many of the settlements in the West Riding dales were made by Irish-Norse colonists a century later. These Vikings were from Norway and they had come via the Shetlands and the west coast of Scotland to found a Viking kingdom around Dublin in the late 9th century. At the beginning of the 10th century they were driven out of Ireland and started settling in Cheshire, Lancashire, the Lake District and eventually in west Yorkshire. They did not settle in the numbers in which the Danes settled the East Riding, and consequently the words they added to the dialect were not as numerous as the number found in the East Riding dialect. Even so, compared with other English dialects, the number of Norse words is huge. There are many Norse words still current throughout Yorkshire as the following list shows: "addle," to earn; "agate," busy with; "fell," hillside; "barn," child; "neave," fist; "beck," stream; "laike," play; "dale," valley; "kirk," church; "ket," rubbish, "lug," ear; "haver," oats; "lig," to lie down; "teem," pour out; "wark," ache; "tig," to touch. These are just a few of the words of Norse origin which are still used widely by dialect speakers—and some people who would not consider themselves dialect speakers—of all three Ridings.

The Norse invasions also added a new set of place-names to the county. The Viking settlers had a flair for administration and divided the large county up into three parts, "thrithjungr" or thriddings, terms which have become distorted in time to "Ridings", sadly lost when they were replaced by the more mundane North, South, East and West Yorkshire. Some indication of Norse/Danish influence on place-names in Yorkshire can be gauged from the figures compiled by the late Prof. A. H. Smith in his survey of Yorkshire place-names in Domesday Book (drawn up about 1085). The North Riding has 28% Norse place-names, the East Riding 40% and in the West Riding, more predominantly Anglian, the percentage drops to 13%, although another 10% are of Anglo-Norse mixture. The Northumbrian Mercian dialects and the languages spoken by the Vikings, Old Norse and Old Danish, were "cousin" languages and the two peoples would be well able to understand each other.

Frequent place-name elements in Yorkshire from the Norse are: "-by" meaning a farmstead, in such words as Denby and Newby; "-scales" meaning a grazing ground, as in Scalebar, Scale Gill and Scholes; Summerscales and Winterscales; "thorpe" meaning an outlying farmstead or settlement, as in Knostrop and Nunthorpe; "-thwaite" meaning a clearing, as in Braithwaite and Micklethwaite; and "-holme" meaning a water meadow, as in Hubberholme and Lawkholme.

Many Norse words are given to natural features. Common Norse words in field names are: "gill," a small ravine; "carr," a marsh; "slack," a hollow; "lund," a small wood; and "rigg," a hill top. There are also a number of Norse derived dialect words for animals and birds which find their way into field and farm names. Some of the more common are: "tewit," a lapwing; "dunnock," a hedgesparrow; "ruddock," a robin; and "laverock," a skylark. The Norse words "gaukr," a cuckoo; "gledr," a hawk; and "ikorno," a squirrel have given the county such place-names as Gawk Stones, Gledhow and Ickornshaw.

When William the Norman landed in 1066, the basis of Yorkshire's dialects and place-names had been laid down. The Viking settlers, while retaining many elements of their Norse vocabulary and features of its pronunciation, soon adopted the dialects of the Angles living in Yorkshire. The formation of early Yorkshire dialects, rich in Scandinavian elements, yet poor in Norse structural features, points to an almost complete and early integration of the English and the Viking folk throughout the county by the time the Norman French came in the 11th century.

Dialects of the
Middle English Period
(1150 - 1450)

IN the fifty or so years before the Conquest, a Dane took the leading role in the government of the country. In 1017 Cnut of Denmark became King of England and his strong rule gave the country a degree of political unity it had never had before. Under succeeding kings, even English kings, like Edward the Confessor, Norse and Danish settlers held high posts in the court and governed large tracts of the North as jarls, known as thanes further south. The result was a firm fixing of Scandinavian elements in English dialects, which survived until the formation of a standard tongue when some of these Norse elements were assimilated into Standard English.

As one would expect there were more Norse elements in the northern dialects than in those further south. The dialects in Yorkshire were a mixed set of Anglo-Norse ones, and in Middle English they became characterised by a gradual dropping of the inflexions of Old English. As a result the dialects of this period became more simple than their predecessors.

There exists one specimen of Yorkshire dialect written in the early 11th century by a Danish settler. It is on an inscription at Aldborough, near Boroughbridge, and it reads:
"Ulf let araeran cyric for hanum and for Gunware saula." In modern English this would read: "Ulf caused a church to he built for himself and for the soul of Gunwaru." Probably the inscription is in a more correct form of Yorkshire dialect than Ulf himself actually spoke; but even so he has made the mistake of putting the Norse "hanum" instead of the English "him."

The areas where the Norsemen settled in large numbers such as Yorkshire, were those in which English grammar became more simplified. This simplifying spread to other dialects and caused the loss of inflexion, which characterises the English language now compared with other European languages.

It may well be that the Yorkshireman's bluntness of expression and the use of as few a words as possible stem from his Norse ancestors. In dialect today it is still common to hear word-endings or whole words, such as the definite article "the," dropped from speech. One hears expressions like, "Yon's Billy Greenwood lad," for "That boy is Billy Greenwood's son." The possessive adjective "its" is frequently abbreviated to "it" as in, "Sitha at yon bairn laikin' wi' it rattil," meaning "Look at that baby playing with its rattle." One classical example of Yorkshire brevity was overheard at a school sports notice-board, where a rather small boy was trying to peer round the broad frame of a friend who played for the school rugby team. "A' ta on?" he asked his larger friend. His question in Standard English meant: "Have you been selected to play in the first fifteen rugby match next Saturday afternoon?" Or the two Yorkshire farmers passing on their tractors in a lane. One said, "Owt?" and the other replied, "Nowt" then drove on. In Standard English their conversation would have gone, "Have you any news?" "No, I haven't anything fresh to report."

The Norman Conquest in 1066 did not materially affect the pronunciation of English dialect speech. Changes that were already apparent long before the Norman-French arrived may have been speeded up with the loss of the English literary tradition as foreign monks filled important roles in the monasteries, the centres of learning. French became the language of the court and the ruling classes, but the English dialects were kept alive not only by illiterate serfs, but also by English nobles. Numerically the Norman-French were never strong enough to oust the English native dialects, but they did add considerably to the vocabulary of English. This is not surprising, since French was the Standard Language of the country along with Latin, which was used in the church. French was taught in the grammar schools, used in the law courts and spoken in parliament until the 14th century, but the English dialects continued to be spoken on the land and in the homes of the English nobility who had to use French or Latin for more formal occasions. By the 13th century most of the educated population would be bi-lingual to a greater or lesser extent and French words also entered the dialects. Many of these medieval French words are still retained in Yorkshire's dialects.

Words originating from the Norman-French invasion of England and the time when French was our standard tongue include "chamer" for a bedroom; "arran," a spider; "to tonse," to brush and comb the hair; "grisomly," grey, covered with smuts; "gallimawfry," a confused mixture; "galivant," to act the fool; "barlow" or "barley," a child's cry meaning to have first choice or be neutral in a game; "cape," top stone but one in a dry-wall; "to cop," to seize; "aumry sole," cupboard bottom; "lowance," mid-morning break; "bonny," beautiful. More recent French words, incidentally, seem to have remained in Yorkshire's dialects when they have disappeared from the standard language— words like "lip-sauve," meaning lip-stick, and "fol-de-rols," the fancy clothes of a woman.

Vocabulary and also pronunciations changed tremendously in Middle English. Middle English is nearer to Modern English than to Old English, though almost 600 years separates us from the late Middle English period and only 300 years divide late Middle English and Old English. The breakdown of the inflexion system in Middle English and new terms introduced by the Normans account for much of this difference, but sounds changed tremendously also. The dialects themselves began to split up further, so that from the early English dialects of Northumbria, Mercia, Kent and Wessex there emerged a new group of speech communities. We classify the Middle English dialects as: Northern dialects, West Midland dialects, East Midland dialects, Central Midland dialects and Southern dialects.

In Yorkshire most of the dialects belong to the Northern group, but there were West Riding dialects which belonged to the West Midland group and shared the characteristics that many of the West Riding dialects south of the Wharfe have today with the dialects of South Lancashire, Cheshire, West Derbyshire, Staffordshire, North Shropshire and West Warwickshire. Anyone wishing to study these sound-changes further should consult the following books which illustrate the change in Yorkshire's dialects during the Middle English period:

A History of English - Barbara M. H. Strang (Methuen + Co)

The Dialect of George Meriton's A Yorkshire Dialogue, C. Dean (Y.D.S. Publications).

An Outline History of the English Language, F. T. Wood (Macmillan).

Modern English and Yorkshire Dialects (1450 - present)

An important feature of dialect change that occurred towards the end of the Middle English Period was the evolution of an English dialect in London that became more frequently used by educated people throughout the country. This dialect was to become the forerunner of modern Standard English. As cultural and economic ties with France broke with the loss of English possessions there, so ties with the French language weakened. No longer was French used as a national Standard Language in England, and by the late 14th century French had ceased to be used in Parliament, law courts and grammar schools as the accepted form of cultured speech. English became again the national tongue of the country.

London, by the beginning of the 14th century, was the established centre of national trade. London dialect at this time was basically a Southern dialect, but as wool was a major export there were many wool merchants living in London who came from the East Midlands, where much of England's wool was produced. The East Midland dialect fused with the Southern dialect to form the basis of the London dialect, which was to become Standard English when it evolved in the 15th century. This new form of Standard Language became used more and more by the merchant, literary and court classes and it developed separately from, but began to influence, the other English dialects. It was used at court and became known as King's English.

During the 15th century regional dialects gradually disappeared from written English, although these dialects continued to have a spoken tradition in poetry and song that lasted until dialect-writing in literature became fashionable again, and not something to be looked down on. The invention of printing also helped the development of the Standard Language and accelerated its separation from the dialects. Books were written and printed in the new fashionable dialect of London; regional dialects, such as those spoken in Yorkshire, tended to become discredited. Authors no longer wrote in their native dialect, but in the educated dialect and more standardised spelling found in books— no longer laboriously copied by hand but the product of the printing press. Printing also helped to spread new words more quickly, so that they became an accepted part of the new standard tongue of the educated, and never entered the dialects except rarely and selectively at later dates. The dialects had become the speech of the illiterate and the uneducated by late Tudor times, but they still retained a peculiar wealth and turn of phrase, which Shakespeare himself used when it suited his purpose better than Standard English.

Dialect speech did not die out completely among the educated classes and it seems doubtful whether for many years educated men from all parts of England ever cleared their speech of regional pronunciation. The speech of the Squire Westerns of the 18th century shows that a Standard English pronunciation was not yet entirely current among the ruling class, though dialect had been relegated to the speech of the uneducated and unsophisticated. Not until the boarding school system was well established in the 19th century did a ruling class lose all trace of its native dialect speech, though regional speech was frowned on in polite circles even as early as the 16th century. Sir Thomas Elyot despairs at some of his aristocratic pupils' speech, the sons of noblemen who learned "a corrupt and foul pronunciation from their nourishers and other foolish women." Yet Sir Walter Raleigh, with all his intellectual accomplishment and courtly habits, never lost his rich

Devon accent and, just a few decades after Raleigh's death, a North Riding lawyer, George Meriton, a highly educated man, was writing again in dialect, Yorkshire dialect, in a long narrative poem he composed to illustrate typical Yorkshire sayings and proverbs in 1673.

Until very recently Yorkshire dialects continued to be frowned upon, more for social than literary or linguistic reasons. There was, however, a continuous flow of Yorkshire dialect literature from George Meriton's time onwards, and in the 18th century Yorkshire dialect-writing continued to flourish in the hands of well-to-do men like Henry Carey and antiquaries like Joseph Ritson. Nineteenth century scholars such as Professor Joseph Wright and Professor F. W. Moorman also continued a long tradition of dialect-study and writing by highly educated people in Yorkshire. Another Leeds University professor and linguistic scholar, J.R.R.Tolkien, even went as far as making up his own dialects in his fantasy novels.

From 1450 to the present day Yorkshire dialect like the Standard Language, has undergone many changes. There was another great vowel change in English in the 18th century, when vowels such as "-er" that had earlier been pronounced "-ar" assumed their modern pronunciation. For example, "deserve" was pronounced "desarve" before the 18th century vowel change. We still have the older pronunciation in Yorkshire dialects for these "-er" words. "Vermin" is an East Riding word for pus and it is pronounced "varmin" by a dialect-speaker. Yet Yorkshire dialect has been influenced by the Standard Language to pronounce "Derby" and "clerk" the way most "er" words are spoken today, when for some reason Standard English pronounces these two words the old way as "Darby" and "clark"!

In the mid-19th century the River Aire was probably the northern boundary of the North Midland dialects. A century later it had encroached as far as somewhere between the Wharfe and Nidd, quite an extensive region, and there are indications that West Riding speech is still moving northwards—a reversal in speech-patterns, it seems, of the population drift south. Perhaps the most influential reason for the advance of the North Midland dialect over the past 200 years is the introduction of industry into the northern dales.

The Industrial Revolution brought to the West Riding vast numbers of rural workers from all over England. Midland farm workers in particular came to seek work in the towns, which were springing up throughout the Riding. As we have seen, there were already pockets of Midland-type place-names in the West Riding established during the period of Mercian occupation in the 7th century during the early Anglian colonisation. The influence of Midland dialects spread as industrialisation spread up and down the dales. What is more, this influence of Midland speech seems to have intensified over the last 100 years.

Regions around Keighley, which are "buffer" zones between the North Midland and true Northern dialects, seemed a 100 years ago to have more Northern elements in them than they have today. Emily Bronte records the Haworth dialect of her day pretty accurately in her novel Wuthering Heights. The character, Old Joseph, speaks nothing else but Haworth dialect throughout the novel and it seems strange to hear him use the Northern dialect form "amang" for the North Midland (and Standard English) form "among." Similarly he uses "lang" for "long" and he is constantly using "gangs" for "goes." which a Haworth dialect speaker today would pronounce as "goes."

The immigration of large numbers of people into the West Riding throughout the 19th century may well account for the very wide variety of dialects spoken between town and town, or even within the larger cities such as Leeds. Allowing for geographical barriers, such as the high Pennine moors between dale and dale, there is still great variation in the speech of villages and towns in the same dale, which are only a few miles apart. The dialects of Bradford, Keighley, Halifax and Huddersfield are different both in speech and to some degree in vocabulary. There is much greater change in dialects over a few miles in the more densely populated West Riding than there is over the same distance in the East and North Ridings.

Finally, city dialects in recent years have followed different lines of development from the dialects in the surrounding rural areas in Yorkshire. The difference between dialect-speakers born and bred in the towns and those who have been brought up in the countryside of the same area is quite pronounced. With the rapid changes this century of all English dialects, it is not surprising that the greatest changes have come in the towns. Extensive changes in social conditions and the speed of life, better means of communication, wider education, two world wars which demanded standard speech of some sort, and media such as radio and television, increased foreign travel—all these have led to dialect change, especially in the towns and cities. Here, too, new trades have developed and old crafts have disappeared so that new standard terms have taken the place of the older dialect terms.

But despite the rapid loss of older dialects, even in the industrial parts of Yorkshire, regional speech is still very different from the Standard Language. Some town dialects are considered more ugly than the traditional country dialects around them. But linguistic beauty lies in the ear of the listener. Doubtless more educated speakers of English in earlier centuries also considered newer types of speech, now universally accepted, equally distasteful to the ear. Industrial dialects in the right context can be just as racy and effective as rural dialects.

Yorkshire's dialects are part of the county's heritage. They have a long and intriguing history, and they have a fine literary tradition that has been carried on from the 7th century, when the poet Caedmon wrote at Whitby, to the present day. The current publications of the Yorkshire Dialect Society reveal just what wealth there is in dialect writing in 20th century Yorkshire. A conversation with any person who has not moved far beyond his birthplace will show dialect is strong in Yorkshire, despite all the powerful influences working against its preservation. An influx of Asian workers beginning in the 1950s has established large Urdu and Bengali speaking communities in the industrial cities and towns, and one wonders what these in the future will contribute to Yorkshire dialect.

Education is currently stimulating new interest in the dialects, and whereas some years ago strong efforts were made to avoid dialect speech and ban it in schools, now it is accepted that the study of dialects can contribute greatly to a deeper understanding of the history and social development of the people who make up Yorkshire's population.

PART TWO
A History of and Selections from Yorkshire Dialect Literature

WE have already mentioned that the oldest ancestor of modern Yorkshire dialects was the speech introduced into northern England by invading Angles of the 5th century. A hundred years later they had sufficiently colonised the land to form their kingdom of Northumbria, a kingdom that embraced the earlier kingdoms of Bernicia, Deira and Elmete. By the end of the 7th century Northumbrian dialect was used throughout Yorkshire, from which the invading Mercians had been driven by Oswi, who reigned from 642—670 AD. Penda, the pagan Mercian king, had been killed by Oswi at the Battle of Winwaed, near Leeds, in 655 AD. Following this battle, the rest of Mercia became Christian and, under Oswi's strong rule, many monasteries were built throughout Northumbria to spread Christianity.

One of these was built by a relative of Oswi at Whitby in 657 AD and was one of seven abbeys founded by Oswi to commemorate his victory over Penda. St. Hild made Whitby Abbey a great centre for the religious leaders of the 7th and 8th centuries, when Northumbria was famous for its literature and culture. It also produced Caedmon, the first known Yorkshire dialect poet, who died somewhere between 670 and 680 AD.

Our sole authority for the fragment of Caedmon's writing which survives (most of his works were probably lost in the Viking attacks on the monasteries in later centuries) is the Anglo-Saxon historian, Bede, who quotes a fraction of Caedmon's *Hymn of the Creation*, in his *Ecclesiastical History*. Caedmon's Hymn is important because it marks the application to new uses of an unwritten oral tradition in Anglian poetry, a tradition which went well back into pagan times when sagas such as Beowulf were composed, being developed from generation to generation by word of mouth by an illiterate population. This oral tradition was put to the service of the Church by Caedmon, who was inspired not by pagan sagas, but by the Old Testament stories and *Lives of the Saints* which were newly circulating among the recently Christianised Angles. Caedmon used old local traditions to make men listen to new Biblical instruction.

In Bede's history we are told that Caedmon was an uneducated herdsman at the monastery of Streoneshalh, the Anglian name for Whitby, which is of later Danish coinage. Bede says that one night, when Caedmon was getting old, he had a dream in which he was divinely inspired to compose a poem about the Creation of the World. Bede then gives a paraphrase of it, which has come to be known as Caedmon's *Hymn*. St. Hild, hearing of Caedmon's verse, had him made a full member of her monastic order and also had him instructed in the Old and New Testaments, which would be taught in Latin. Everything he learned from Latin he turned into verse, in his own dialect. Bede says:

"He sang the creation of the world, the origin of man and all the history of Genesis; the departure of the children of Israel out of Egypt, their entrance into the Promised Land; and many other histories from holy scripture; the Incarnation, Passion, Resurrection of our Lord, and His Ascension into Heaven; the coming of the Holy Ghost, and the teaching of the Apostles. Likewise he composed many songs about the terror of future judgements; as well as many more about the blessings and judgements of God, by all of which he endeavoured to draw men away from the love of sin, and to excite in them devotion to well-doing and persevering in doing good."

Caedmon has been acknowledged by some scholars as the author of several surviving anonymous Old English poems, but this is by no means certain. He obviously composed many more poems than the *Hymn* from Bede's account of his life, but these were lost in the destruction of Northumbria and its culture by the Vikings in the late 8th and 9th centuries. However, he is universally acknowledged the author of the *Hymn of the Creation*, of which only eighteen half-lines survive. The old English poets wrote their verse in half-lines; lines which did not rhyme but were united by regular stress and alliteration and assonance, the repetition of similar sounding consonants and vowels.

Below is Bede's version of Caedmon's *Hymn* in the original Old English, together with a modern translation later in Bede's account of how the passage came to be composed:

Nu we sculon herigean	Heonfonrices Weard,
Meotodes meahte	ond his modgethanc,
weore Wuldorfaeder,	swa he wundra gehwaes,
ece Drihten,	or onstalde.
He aerest sceop	eorthan bearnum
Heofon to hrofe,	halig Scyppend;
tha middangeard	moncynnes Weard,
ece Drihten	aefter teode,
firum foldan	Frea aelmihtig.

It is quite a far fetch from modern Yorkshire dialect, but this is what the dialect spoken by the Angles in Yorkshire looked like, and surprisingly enough there is the odd word here still used in current Yorkshire dialect. The word "nu," in Old English, means "now" in Modern Standard English; yet dialect-speakers in north and east Yorkshire still pronounce it the Anglian way and say "nu." Again, there is the word "bearnum" which means "children." Yorkshire people still use the word "barn" or "bairn" for a child, and "father" in some parts of Yorkshire is still pronounced "fader," just as the Angles pronounced it in "Wuldorfaeder," father of Glory. If you look closely at other words in the Old English version, you will see their equivalents in use today in the modernised version below.

Caedmon is an important poet for the students of Yorkshire dialect, because he set the traditional pattern for many dialect-writers who followed him. Like Caedmon they were often artisans and uneducated men and some of them, like Caedmon were illiterate at first, composing their verse orally and getting others to write it down for them. Like Caedmon's verse, the impact of their writing comes from its very simplicity and the peculiar appeal dialect words have to those who use and understand them. (Nearly always the forcefulness of dialect-writing is lost once it is turned into Standard English.)

Bede's account of how Caedmon was inspired to write poetry runs as follows:

"This man (Caedmon) had lived an ordinary life till he had reached old age. He had never learned a song, and so, often at the feast, when it was the time for entertaining and each in turn had to sing to the harp; and when Caedmon saw his turn approaching for the harp, then in shame he arose from the banquet and went home to his house. Once, when he had done this, and left the feasting-hall to go to the cow-shed (for the care of the cattle was entrusted him that night) and had laid down to sleep there, a man appeared to him and greeted him, calling him by his name: 'Caedmon, sing me something.' Then he answered, 'I cannot sing, and so I left the feasting and came hither because I could not sing.' The man spoke to him again and said, 'Nevertheless, thou canst sing to me.' Caedmon said, 'What am I to sing?' and he replied, 'Sing me the Creation.' Immediately Caedmon received that command he began to sing in praise of God the Creator, verses and words he had never heard before. This is the order of them:

Now we must praise	the Guardian of Heaven,
the might of God	and his mind,
the work of the Gloryfather,	since he performed wonders,
the eternal Lord;	the beginning
He first shaped	for the children of the earth
the heavens as their roof,	the holy Creator;
then this middle-earth	the Guardian of mankind,
the eternal Lord,	afterwards adorned
the earth for men,	the Prince almighty.

Then Caedmon rose up from sleep and clearly remembered all he had sung while he slept, and straightaway added in the same rhythm many words of a song worthy of God."

Between the 7th and the 14th centuries there must have been many pieces of literature composed in Yorkshire, but few have come down to us. As we have seen from the historical events outlined in Part I of this book, the period between the 7th and the 14th centuries was one of great upheaval, especially in Yorkshire and the North of England. Great social upheavals were constantly taking place, first with the invasion and settlement of Yorkshire by the Vikings, and then by the Normans. The Vikings destroyed a flourishing literary Northumbrian tradition in the north, and the centre of Anglo-Saxon culture moved south, to Wessex, the kingdom of Alfred, which preserved and fostered the traditions laid down in the north. Pagan Norse culture superseded for a time the more sophisticated Anglian culture in Yorkshire, whose identity as a county, however, was founded by the Danes and Norsemen and whose speech changed under the influence of their tongue.

Eventually, Old English itself was drastically altered after the Norman invasion, and French culture for a time pushed native speech and literature into the background, as French monks took charge of many of the monasteries, which were the centres of learning. Little that was written in English between 1100 and 1300 is of great literary value, but once the Norman-French language and the Anglo-Norse tongues had fused, a new form of English, Middle English, produced some fine writing again; and Middle English, like Old English, was still a language of dialects, the standard languages being French and Latin.

After Caedmon, the next great Yorkshire writer was Richard Rolle, a mystic and a hermit, who wrote some fine religious lyrics in both prose and poetry. Richard Rolle was born at Thornton-le-Dale, near Pickering. He went to Oxford University but returned to Yorkshire without taking religious orders and became a hermit. He did not cut himself off entirely from human companionship. His patrons were Sir John and Lady Dalton, who gave him a cell on their estate. Later in his life he went to live at Hampole, north of Doncaster, where he died in 1349, the year of the Black Death.

He is an important figure in Middle English literature because he inspired writings of devotional piety and his works were frequently imitated long after his death. Many of his writings have a strong emotional content rather than an intellectual one (another feature of Yorkshire dialect-writing) yet there is a sincerity about them, which made him such a powerful figure in an age when the Church in general suffered from apathy. One feature of Rolle's dialect, incidentally, is a marked lack of inflexions in his language, which is characteristic of Modern English, and different from the other English dialects of his day. This last verse, from a poem he wrote, *Love is Life*, illustrates the simple beauty of his poetry:

"Iesu es lufe that lastes ay, til Him es owre langyng;
Iesu the nyght turnes to the day, the dawnyng intil spryng.
Iesu, thynk on us now and ay, for Thee we halde oure keyng;
Iesu, gyf us grace, as Thou wel may, to luf Thee withouten endyng."

"Jesus is love that lasts always, to Him is our longing;
Jesus the night turns to the day, the dawn into full morning.
Jesus, think of us now and always, for Thee we hold our king;
Jesus, give us grace, as Thou well may, to love Thee without ending."

This form of English is much more like our own than that of Caedmon. The effect of Norse on Yorkshire dialect is clearly seen, for it has lost nearly all the complicated endings and the inflexions it had in Old English. However, the Middle English word " in the first line, is still current in east Yorkshire dialect meaning "to," and in the West Riding as "tul," e.g. "Ah gave it tul 'im." The phrase "think on" in the third line is also used currently in Yorkshire dialect in the sense of to "think of," or "remember" e.g. "Ah've thowt on it oft" meaning, "I've thought of it often." and "Nah, think on what tha's got to do" meaning " Now, remember what you've got to do."

The Middle English period is also an important period in the development of Yorkshire dialect literature for it is in this period that the first dramatic writings appear, the York and Wakefield Mystery Plays. These plays—or more correctly pageants—were short dramas acted by members of various trade guilds as episodes in a complete cycle performed on Corpus Christi Day. They are, of course, religious in origin and derive from earlier Continental and Latin liturgical plays, which were performed inside the early medieval churches to illustrate biblical stories. It seems possible also that there were other plays written in the dialect, secular plays from which the St. George playlets derive. These are still acted in many parts of Yorkshire, especially in schools, as mummers' plays. *The Yorkshire Pace Egg Play*, performed mainly in the Halifax and Calder Valley area, is also in the tradition of the medieval plays of the 15th century.

The York cycle is one of the highlights of the cultural scene in York each year. *The First Shepherd's Play* from the Wakefield Cycle is also performed frequently as a Nativity Play. The current popularity of these plays, especially when combined with musical interludes, speaks highly of their content as pieces of skilful drama. Both Cycles have as their central themes the concept of Christian salvation and were performed out of doors around Whitsun, when the weather was most favourable. The York Mystery Cycle is first heard of in 1376 and by the early 15th century the town authorities, not the churches, were in charge of the productions of the plays, with trade guilds financing the production of the individual pageants. Sometimes they vied with each other in producing the pageants most splendidly, for the biblical episodes chosen by each guild were designed to represent the skills of its trade.

Each pageant would be acted by members of the guild moving in procession around the town, or its walls, from one station to another. Consequently, the plays were performed on wagons which could be towed from station to station, the actors preparing and dressing themselves underneath the wagons before appearing on the floor of the wagon above, which formed the stage. Little is known about the authors of the plays, which were probably improvised or added to at each production, but it is certain that their authors were Yorkshiremen and, in *The First Shepherd's Play* of the Wakefield Cycle, Yorkshire character and wit is caught exquisitely by the anonymous author in the dramatic persons of the shepherds and their droll antics, as well as their interest in music.

As Part I of this book has shown ("Modern English" section) in the 15th and 16th centuries there was a rapid spread throughout the country of the London dialect. This new type of standard language, later known as "King's English," did not stamp out the English dialects as spoken forms of the language, but it pushed dialect-writing very much into the background for a time.

One form of dialect literature which escaped the influence of Standard English was song and ballad, handed down orally among the uneducated countryfolk in much the same way as Old English and Norse sagas were passed on from generation to generation. The further away from London a region lay, the stronger was the retention of regional literature and speech. The north of England, in common with the Scottish lowlands, retained many traditional songs and ballads when regions nearer London were eager to rid themselves of their provincialisms and use the language of the court for their writings.

Yorkshire did not entirely escape from this influence. A popular song during Elizabeth I's reign was *York, York, for my Monie*, first published in 1584. It epitomises a Yorkshireman's pride in his county, yet it is written in Standard English and shows no trace of dialect. In 1615 Richard Braithwaite also wrote a poem called *The Yorkshire Cottoneers*; he, too, used the standard tongue, though he dedicated it to "all true-bred Northerne Sparks, of the generous society of the Cottoneers, who hold their High-roade by the Pinder of Wakefield, the Shoo-maker of Bradford, and the white Coate of Kendall." Other songs with Yorkshire themes were written about the same time, notable of which were the sensational street ballads composed about the Calverley murders in 1605. (These murders also inspired the Jacobean play, *A Yorkshire Tragedie*, in which Shakespeare himself had a hand in 1608.) But Yorkshire dialect clearly did not have the appeal it once had two centuries earlier.

A traditional Yorkshire ballad that survived this standardising period of the language was *The Cleveland Lyke Wake Dirge*. It appears in a publication of 1686, which refers to its composition in a much earlier time; indeed, some critics have seen elements in this dirge which are of pre-Christian origin and go back to Celtic times. The dirge was sung at funerals or over a corpse during its lying-in period before burial, and until well into the 17th century a woman was hired as a professional mourner to sing this dirge. (Professional mourners were hired for funerals in Yorkshire right down to the 19th century, when they were graced—in the West Riding at any rate—with the name of "bawlers"!) The idea of the soul, after death, making a journey through some sort of purgatorial region on the moors forms the essence of the poem, and in this respect the dirge has a theme which is common to Jewish and Middle Eastern myths. The version here is that of the earliest known one taken from John Aubrey's *"Remains of Gentilisme and Judaisme,"* published in 1686.

Cleveland Lyke-Wake Dirge

This ean night, this ean night,
Every night and awle:
Fire and Fleet and Candle-leet,
And Christ receive thy Sawle.

When thou from hence dost pass away,
Every night and awle:
To Whinny-moor thou comest at last,
And Christ receive thy Sawle.

If ever thou gave either hosen or shoon,
Every night and awle,
Sitt thee downe and putt them on,
And Christ receive thy Sawle.

But if hosen or shoon thou never gave nean,
Every night and awle;
The Whinnes shall prick thee to the bare beane,
And Christ receive thy Sawle.

From Whinny-moor that thou mayst pass,
Every night and awle,
To Brig o' Dread thou comest at last,
And Christ receive thy Sawle.

From Brig o' Dread that thou mayst pass,
Every night and awle,
To Purgatory fire thou com'st at last,
And Christ receive thy Sawle.

If ever thou gave either Milke or Drinke,
Every night and awle,
The fire shall never make thee shrink,
And Christ receive thy Sawle.

But of milk or drink thou never gave nean,
Every night and awle,
The Fire shall burn thee to the bare beane,
And Christ receive thy Sawle.

ean—one.
fleet—floor.
shoon—shoes.
beane—bone.
Brig o' Dread—the Bridge of Dread.

Yorkshire dialect after about 1650 was once more used as a means of literary expression, springing from rather different motives than the medieval writings. The latter part of the 17th century marks the beginning of many movements which characterise modem life. Scientific investigation was one of these movements, when men like Harvey were researching into medicine and Newton into physics. It was the era when the Royal Society was founded, the era of the antiquary who dabbled in many branches of learning, including language, as well as the natural sciences. Intelligent country gentlemen and squires began to dabble in archaeology and set up local history collections in their manor houses as a kind of status symbol, and some of these well-to-do antiquaries also began to study and collect expressions in the dialect from the areas they lived in.

John Ray, as famous a naturalist as he was a philologist, was one such antiquary. He collected plants and dialect words and expressions. In 1674 he published *A Collection of English Words*, 'not generally used, with their Significations and Original, in two Alphabetical Catalogues, the one of such as are proper to the Northern, the other to the Southern Counties.' He corresponded closely with Ralph Thoresby, the Leeds historian, who sent him a list of Leeds and district dialect words in April 1703. The Rev. Francis Brokesby, Rector of Rowley in the East Riding, had supplied him with similar information in 1691.

As Ray collected his dialect material, there appeared two important poems in Yorkshire dialect, the first known Yorkshire dialect poems to be composed since the formation of Standard English. They are called *A Yorkshire Dialogue*, and later versions are attributed to George Meriton, a North Riding lawyer from Northallerton. There are three versions of the later dialogue. The first dialogue had been published in 1673 as a broadsheet at York, and the versions of the later one appeared in 1683, with additions in 1685 and 1697.

In the tradition of the other antiquaries of his day, George Meriton did not confine his studies to dialect alone, for he wrote works on legal topics and also penned historical, satirical and moral treatises. The interest which Meriton's *Dialogue* holds for the modern student of Yorkshire dialect literature is twofold. Firstly his *Dialogue* is the earliest known example of modern Yorkshire dialect, as distinct from the Middle English dialect of the Miracle Plays and Rolle's verse; secondly, it possesses all the earthly realism of Yorkshire rural life in the 17th century about which the poem paints a very vivid picture. Meriton, in so far as he deliberately includes many popular Yorkshire proverbs of his day in the poem, is also the forerunner of a line of Yorkshire scholars applying serious study to the history of dialect and language in succeeding centuries. He pre-dates by nearly a century the writing in dialect which Burns was to make so popular.

Meriton's *Dialogue* is based on the conversation of seven characters. The title of his work explains what it is to be about: "A Yorkshire Dialogue in its pure Natural Dialect, as it (is) now commonly spoken in the North parts of Yorkshire, being Miscellaneous discourse, or Hotchpotch of several Country affaires, begun by a Daughter and her Mother and continued by the Father, Son, Uncle, Niece and land-Lord." Meriton quite clearly delights in his native dialect and the lore of the area in which he was reared, for he never misses an opportunity of inserting a wide variety of proverbs which were current in North Yorkshire during his lifetime—proverbs such as: "There's no Carrion will kill a Crawe"; "Neare is my sarke (shirt), but nearer is my skin"; "A curst cow hes short horns"; "Change of pastures maks fat cawves (calves), but change of women maks lean knaves"; and "they that Wed before they're Wise will dee before they Thrive."

Despite the poem's obvious defects, such as abrupt changes of topic and sometimes a too deliberate and clumsy attempt to force in a proverb, the *Dialogue* is a fine piece of dialect-writing. It has vitality and it has an unabashed wit which is essentially Yorkshire and readily finds expression in North Riding dialect. Though one of the first examples of English dialect verse written in modern dialect, Meriton's *Dialogue* still holds its own with any dialect-writing that has appeared in subsequent centuries and it is well worth the effort to read it today.

The next known piece of dialect-writing after Meriton's verse is a song, written in Yorkshire dialect, which appeared in a popular 18th century ballad-opera called *A Wonder*, or *An Honest Yorkshireman*. (It seems people outside the county were more canny of the Tyke than they are today; possibly because Yorkshire horse-dealers brought a deal of notoriety upon themselves as they travelled the country selling horses.) The opera, written not long after John Gay's *Beggars' Opera*, and similar in tone, was written by Henry Carey in 1736. Carey is remembered better for his poem *Sally in our Alley*, but one song from his opera is a good piece of dialect verse, written in North Riding dialect and called:

An Honest Yorkshireman

I is i' truth a coontry youth,
Nean used to Lunnon fashions;
Yet vartue guides, an' still presides
Ower all my steps and passions.
Nea coortly leer, bud all sincere,
Nea bribes shall ivver blinnd me;
If thoo can like a Yorkshire tike,
A rogue thoo'll nivver finnd me.

Thof envy's tongue, so slimly hung,
Would lee aboot oor coonty,
Nea men o' t' earth boast greater worth,

Or mair extend their boonty.
Orr northern breeze wi' us agrees,
An' does for wark weel fit us;
I' public cares, an' love affairs,
Wi' honour we acquit us.

Sea greeat a maand is ne'er confaand
Tiv onny shire or nation,
They gie un meast praise whea weel displays
A larned eddication;
Whaal rancour rolls i' laatle souls,
By shallow views dissarnin',
They're nobbut wise 'at awlus prize
Good manners, sense an' larnin'.

nean—not; Lunnon—London; nea—no; thof —though; lee—lie; wark—work; weel—well; greeat—great; maand—mind; confaand—confined; gie—give; laatle—little; nobbut—only; awlus—always.

Another Yorkshire poem, *Snaith Marsh*, appearing about 1754, is written in east Yorkshire dialect at a time when the Enclosure Movement was affecting the East and North Ridings, the great arable farmlands of Yorkshire. The Enclosure Acts in the 18th century had little effect on the moorland and hilly commons of the West Riding, but enclosure of much good grazing land to the east and north of the county produced a great deal of hardship for the smallholding farmers there. (Oliver Goldsmith's famous poem, *The Deserted Village*, written in 1770, shows in a similar fashion how enclosure was adversely affecting other parts of rural England.)

Snaith Marsh is written mainly in Standard English but towards the end of his poem the anonymous Yorkshire writer begins to use more and more dialect, especially in the concluding section, in which the Snaith farmer sees himself ruined in fortune by the enclosure of nearby common land, Snaith Marsh, and ruined in heart by the desertion of his betrothed to a more prosperous rival, Roger:

Alas! will Roger e'er his sleep forgo,
Afore larks sing, or early cocks 'gin crow,
As I've for thee, ungrateful maiden, done,
To help thee milking, e'er day wark begun?
And when thy well-stripp'd kye would yield no more,
Still on my head the reeking kit I bore.
And, oh! bethink thee, then, what lovesome talk
We've held together, ganging down the baulk,
Maund'ring at time which would na for us stay,
But now, I ween, maes no such haste away.
Yet, O! return eftsoon and ease my woe,
And to some distant parish let us go,
And there again them leetsome days restore
Where, unassail'd by meety folk in power,
Our cattle yet may feed, tho' Snaith Marsh be no more.
But wae is me! I wot I fand am grown,
Forgetting Susan is already gone,
And Roger aims e'er Lady Day to wed;
The banns last Sunday in the church were bid.
But let me, let me first i' t' churchyard lig,
For soon I there must gang, my grief's so big.
All others in their loss some comfort find;
Though Ned's like me reduc'd, yet Jenny's kind,
And though his fleece no more our parsons taks,
And roast goose, dainty food, our table lacks,
Yet he, for tithes ill paid, gets better land,
While I am ev'ry way o' t' losing hand.
My adlings wared, and yet my rent to pay,
My geese, like Susan's faith, flown far away;

My cattle, like their master, lank and poor,
My heart with hopeless love to pieces tore,
And all these sorrows came syne Snaith Marsh was no more.

well-stripp'd kye—well milked cows; reeking kit—steaming milk pail; ganging—going; baulk—cowshed gangway; maundering—grumbling; ween—think; maes—makes; meety— mighty; wot—think; fond—foolish, mad; hg—lie; adhings wared—earnings are spent; syne—since.

There are several other Yorkshire dialect poems which can be attributed to the 18th century, but my own favourite is an anonymous one called *I'm Yorkshire Too*, which is very similar in style to Henry Carey's poem but richer in puns and subtler in humour. Its theme is a common one even today—that of the Tyke who is impressed by the glories of London on his first visit there, but not so impressed that he is taken in by the city-slickers of the capital, some of whom are expatriate Yorkshiremen.

"I'm Yorkshire Too"

By t' side of a brig, that stands ower a brook,
I was sent betimes to school;
I went wi the stream, as I studied my book,
An' was thought to be no small fool;
I never yet bowt a pig in a poke,
For, to give Awd Nick his due,
Tho' oft I've dealt wi' Yorkshire folk,
Yet I was Yorkshire, too.

I was pretty well liked by each village maid,
At races, wake or fair,
For my father had addled a vast in trade,
And I were his son and heir.
And seeing that I didn't want for brass,

Poor girls came first to woo,
But tho' I delight in a Yorkshire lass,
Yet I was Yorkshire, too!

To Lunnon by father I was sent,
Genteeler manners to see;
But fashion's so dear, I came back as I went,
And so they made nothing o' me.
My kind relations would soon have found out
What was best wi' my money to do:
Says I, 'My dear cousins, I thank ye for nowt,
But I'm not to be cozen'd by you,
For I am Yorkshire, too!'

brig—bridge; *Awd Nick*—the devil; *wake*—holiday; *addled a vast in trade*—earned a lot in business.

The Wensleydale Lad is another poem probably composed during the late 18th century because in one of the stanzas there is a reference to a King George, one of the Hanoverian kings. It is an interesting poem despite its anonymity for, like many Yorkshire dialect poems, through it, we receive odd glimpses of social life and the social attitudes of earlier generations of Yorkshiremen.

The hero of the poem, a Wensleydale farmer's son, goes off on the spree, not to London, but to Leeds—itself a metropolis to the raw country lad up for the day to enjoy himself. His comments about Leeds are amusing, but they are also interesting, for they concern a Leeds which was changing under the influence of the Industrial Revolution from a small country market town to a highly industrialised and commercial city. Indeed, the first object which catches the Wensleydale lad's eye is a factory, a completely new phenomenon to the farmer's son. The sophisticated machines there baffle him, as he is familiar only with basic agricultural tools, and he comments on an early steam-engine, "Old Ned," installed in a Leeds flax mill.

"The Wensleydale Lad"

When I were at home wi' my fayther an' mother, I niver had na fun;
They kept me goin' frae morn to neet, so I thowt frae them I'd run.
Leeds Fair were coomin' on, an' I thowt I'd have a spree,
So I put on my Sunday cooat an' went right merrily.

First thing I saw were t' factory, I niver seed one afore;
There were threads an' tapes, an' tapes an' silks, to sell by
                                      monny a score.
Owd Ned turn's iv'ry wheel, an' iv'ry wheel a strap;
"Begor!" says I to t' maister-man, "Owd Ned's a rare strong chap."

Next I went to Leeds Owd Church—I were niver i' one i' my days,
An' I were maistly ashamed o' misel, for I didn't knaw their ways;
There were thirty or forty folk, i' tubs an' boxes sat,
When up cooms a saucy owd fellow. Says he, "Noo, lad, take
                                        off thy hat."

Then in there cooms a great Lord Mayor, an' over his
                                      shooders a club,
An, he gat into a white sack-poke, an gat into t' topmost tub.
An' then there cooms anither chap, I thinks they call'd him Ned,
An' he gat into t' bottommost tub, an' mock'd all t' other chap said.

So they began to preach an' pray, they prayed for George, oor King;
When up jumps t' chap i' t' bottommost tub. Says he, "Good
                                      folks, let's sing."
I thowt some sang varra weel, while others did grunt an' groan,
Ivery man sang what he wad, so I sang "Darby an' Joan."

When preachin' an' prayin' were over, an' folks were gangin' away,
I went to t' chap i' t' topmost tub. Says I, "Lad, what's to pay?"
"Why, nowt," says he, "my lad." Begor! I were right fain,
So I click'd hod o' my gret club stick an' went whistlin' oot again.

seed—saw; Owd Ned—possibly the nickname for an early steam-engine; Begor—by God!; maister-man—mill-master, Leeds Owd Church—Leeds Parish Church; tubs an' boxes —pulpits and pews; shooders—shoulders; sack-poke—cornsack; clicked hod— took hold.

An anthology of Yorkshire poetry was published by Joseph Ritson in 1786, but none of it is really in dialect, though all the poems have Yorkshire themes. However, British dialect-writing towards the end of the 18th century received a great fillip through the works of Robert Burns (whose Lowland Scottish dialect, incidentally, is directly related to the North and East Riding dialects). It is not surprising, therefore, that a sample of Yorkshire dialect poetry appears four years after Burns' death in 1796, for in 1800 a posthumous collection of poems, *Poems on Several Occasions*, appeared which had been written by the Rev. Thomas Browne, a schoolmaster and journalist who edited *The Hull Advertiser* from 1797 to 1798. He died in 1798 but his friends published a collection of his verse in 1800 in honour of his memory.

Most of the poems are written in Standard English but at the end of the collection appears a section called *Specimens of the Yorkshire Dialect*, which contains five poems. In contrast to his poems written in Standard English, which are conventional types of late 17th century verse, Thomas Browne's dialect poetry is original and racy. He depicts vividly the life he saw around him in East Yorkshire towns and villages. His song *When I was a wee laatle totterin' bairn* captures the feelings of an East Riding country girl who is impatiently awaiting the day of the local fair, when she plans to escape from an overbearing, nattering mother by eloping with her sweetheart, who has been secretly courting her on Saturday nights. The age-old expressions of independence of the young are well-caught in this short but effective song of three stanzas. The headstrong teenager at odds with her mother is by no means a modern characteristic in Yorkshire!

Another interesting feature of Thomas Browne's dialect verse is that it reflects more strongly than his Standard English verse the effects of the Romantic Movement in poetry, which had just made its impact on English literature. Browne was a contemporary of Wordsworth and Coleridge and in the spontaneity and naturalness of its language, Browne's poetry shows its affinity with the Romantic Age which had dawned.

A Song

When I was a wee laatle totterin' bairn,
    An' had nobbud just gitten short frocks,
When to gang I at first was beginnin' to lairn,
    On my brow I gat monny hard knocks.
For sae waik, an' sae silly an' helpless was I
    I was always a tumblin' doon then,
While my mother would twattle me gently an' cry,
    "Honey Jenny, tak care o' thisen."

When I grew bigger, an' got to be strang,
    'At I cannily ran all about
By misen, whor I liked, then I always mud gang
    Bithout bein' tell'd about ought;
When, however, I com to be sixteen year awd,
    An' rattled an' ramp'd amang men,
My mother would call o' me in an' would scaud,
    An' cry—"Huzzy, tak care o' thisen."

> I've a sweetheart cooms noo upo' Setterday nights,
>   An' he swears at he'll mak me his wife;
> My mam grows sae stingy, she scauds an' she flytes,
> An' twitters me oot o' my life.
> Bud she may leuk sour, an' consait hersen wise,
>   An' preach agean likin' young men;
> Sen I's grown a woman her clack I'll despise,
>   An' I's marry!—tak care o' misen.

laatle—little; *bairn*—child; *nobbud*—only; *to gang*—to go, to walk; *waik*—weak; *twattle*—prattle to; *At*—so that; *cannily*—carefully; *Bithout*—without; *scaud*—scold; *stingy*—bitter; *flytes*—argues; *twitters*—worries; *consait*—consider; *sen*—since; *clack*—empty talk; *I's*—I shall.

Perhaps the most important feature of Browne's dialect poems is the amount of interest they aroused in dialect writing throughout Yorkshire. Earlier poems, like Meriton's *Dialogue*, seem to have been written for a very limited audience, possibly more as an academic exercise on the part of the author or on momentary personal whim rather than for a general readership. By the early 19th century the printing of books was cheaper than it had been a hundred years before, and booksellers throughout Yorkshire—a county rapidly expanding in population as the Industrial Revolution gained impetus—were quick to take advantage of the interest shown in Thomas Browne's dialect verse. Browne's works, therefore, reached a much wider audience than any dialect writer's works had reached before, and his writings remained popular among a wide section of Yorkshire society throughout the 19th century as literacy improved.

When the population grew so rapidly in the West Riding towns, especially during the 19th century, a new feature in Yorkshire dialect writing appeared. As literacy progressed among the working classes the worker-poet was created. Up to the 19th century most dialect-writers like George Meriton and Thomas Browne had been well educated men. Some of them like Henry Carey had been writers by profession. But with the advent of industry came universal education, tenuous at first. Sunday Schools, then later Mechanics' Institutes and finally the state Board Schools, provided education which became accessible to more and more of the working classes. With education came literacy; with literacy, writing—original writing expressed in the native dialects of the working classes.

Before the 19th century the farm labourer and rural pursuits had often been the subject of dialect verse composed by educated men, but during the 19th century the farm labourer himself and his urban counterpart began writing in dialect. It is logical that many of these early worker poets should find the writings of Robert Burns a natural source of inspiration. Throughout the century, the influence of Burns is seen again and again in the works of Yorkshire dialect writers from the time of David Lewis, probably the first worker-poet who wrote at the beginning of the century and died in 1858, right down to William Wright (1836-97), the bohemian Keighley dialect poet who not only imitated many of Bums' poems but dressed like the Scot in plaid shawl and tam o' shanter!

David Lewis was a Knaresborough gardener who became a schoolmaster later on in life. Probably because of the interest in dialect Thomas Browne's poems stimulated, Lewis was able to publish a collection of verse called *The Landscape and Other Poems*, at York in 1815, the year of Waterloo. Like Browne's collection, some of Lewis's poems are in Standard English, but they are by not as high a quality as Browne's poems; nevertheless, they are possibly of greater interest because Lewis was a self-taught man, and he was the earliest known worker-poet to use modem Yorkshire dialect in his writings. His *Elegy on the Death of a Frog* shows his indebtedness to Burns, for it bears a strong resemblance in theme and expression to Burns' *To a Mouse*.

Elegy on the Death of a Frog (1815)

Ya summer day when I were mowin',
When flooers of monny soorts were growin'
Which fast befoor my scythe fell bowin',
    As I advance,
A frog I cut widout my knowin'—
    A sad mischance.

Poor luckless frog, why com thoo here?
Thoo sure were destitute o' fear;
Some other way could thoo nut steer
    To shun the grass?
For noo that life, which all hod dear,
    Is gean, alas!

Hadst thoo been freeten'd by the soond
With which the mowers strip the groond,
Then fled away wi' nimble boond,
    Thoo'd kept thy state:
But I, unknawin', gay a wound,
    Which browt thy fate.

Sin thoo com frae thy parent spawn,
Wi' painted cooat mair fine than lawn,
And golden rings round baith ees drawn,
    All gay an' blithe,
Thoo lowpt the fields like onny fawn,
    But met the scythe.

Frae dikes where winter watters stead
Thoo corn unto the dewy mead,
Regardless of the cattle's treead,
    Wi' pantin' breeath,
For to restore thy freezin' bleead,
    But met wi' deeath.

A Frenchman early seekin' prog,
Will oftentinmes ransack the bog,
To finnd a sneel, or weel-fed frog,
    To give relief;
But I prefer a leg of hog,
    Or roond o' beef.

But liker far to the poor frog
I's wanderin' through the world for prog,
Where deeath gies monny a yan a jog,
    An' cuts them doon;
An' though I think misen incog,
    That way I's boun.

Time whets his scythe and shakes his glass,
And though I know all flesh be grass,
Like monny mair I play the ass,
    Don't seem to know;
But here wad sometime langer pass,
    Befoor I go.

Ye bonnie lasses, livin' flooers,
Of cottage mean, or gilded booers,
Possessed of attractive pooers,
    Ye all mun gang
Like frogs in meadows fed by shooers,
    Ere owt be lang.

> Though we to stately plant be grown,
> He easily can mow us doon;
> It may be late, or may be soon,
> > His scythe we feel;
> Or is it fittin' to be known?
> > Therefore fareweel.

Ya—one; *flooers*—flowers; *hod*—hold; *gean*—gone; *baith ees*—both eyes; *low pt*—leaped; *dikes*—ditches; *steead*—stood; *prog*—food; *roond*—round; *yan*—one; *incog*—unknown; *boun*—going; *booers*—bowers.

David Lewis's verse is also significant because it marks the emergence of West Riding dialect-poetry, which, as the 19th century progressed, was to build up a tradition of its own verse and themes quite separate from the dialect writing of the other two Ridings. Although it seems likely that the popularity gained for Yorkshire dialect writing by Browne's and Lewis's verse in the early decades of the 19th century gave an undoubted stimulus to West Riding dialect writers, as the century progressed West Riding writers switched from writing about rural themes and rustic customs to expressing their views on the features of the growing towns and cities.

The population explosion in the late 18th century and throughout the 19th century radically altered the nature and dialects of the West Riding. In the mid-18th century there were only about 360,000 people in the whole of the West Riding; scattered in small market towns, villages and hamlets whose industries were all by hand. Sheffield cutlers and Bradford weavers alike pursued their crafts using hand-operated machinery. Leeds in the mid-18th century had a population of just over 7,000 and was famous as a market town for cloth produced higher up the dales. A hundred years later, in 1861, the population of Leeds was 207,000. In 1901 it was 428,000—far larger than the population of the entire Riding 150 years earlier.

This rate of phenomenal growth was the pattern for all West Riding towns and cities in the 19th century, but unfortunately social conditions did not keep pace with population growth and the most abysmal slums, working and living conditions came in the wake of the Industrial Revolution. The works of the West Riding dialect writers reflect these terrible changes. Throughout their prose and poetry the evils of the factory system (child labour, poverty, and a high death rate) occur again and again. Their writings capture the depressing state of existence they had to endure as few writings in the Standard Language capture it. Their dialect writing is the more poignant because many of these worker-poets themselves suffered the conditions they express in their verse and prose.

The great influx of workers from all over the country and Ireland into the West Riding produced a wider variety of dialects, so that today there is a distinct difference in dialect speech between one West Riding town and another, although they all belong to the same family of English dialects, the North Midland group. There are dialect differences, too, in the smallest of towns. For example, in the old Borough of Keighley, (now part of Bradford Met) at the head of Airedale, there are dialects in the Worth Valley villages which are quite distinguishable from the dialects spoken across the Aire Valley at Riddlesden and Morton, or a few miles further up the Pennines at Cowling and Silsden.

The reason why the first West Riding dialect writers were self-educated workers and not educated scholars, like those in the East and North Ridings, may lie in the fact that West Riding dialects were frowned upon by the 19th century middle-class, particularly the womenfolk, who did much to eradicate them from their own speech. It may well have been that the Bradford millmaster or Sheffield steel-man, who had himself come up in the world from the ranks of the working class, did not want his children speaking like his workers. Speaking some form of Standard English distanced him and his family from them. For a long time dialect speech—and writing—was frowned upon as a social stigma, and this attitude has not yet disappeared, alas, among the unenlightened and uneducated!

John James, the first historian of Bradford, writing in 1866 in his *History of Bradford*, captures well the attitude prevalent among his own class during the mid-19th century:

"The dialect of the inhabitants of this district is marked with strong peculiarities, similar to those which prevail in the parish of Halifax and in Lancashire. The peculiar corruption which I have observed in the dialect here, is in the pronunciation of the vowel 'o' and the diphthong 'oo'; they are almost invariably pronounced as if written with an 'i' immediately after them—as coal pronounced 'coil'; hole, 'hoil'; school, 'schooil'; noon, 'noin'. The greater part of the other vowels and diphthongs are also perverted in the pronunciation, but the larger number of these corruptions may be found in the dialect of the inhabitants of the whole of the western and northern parts of Yorkshire... . These barbarisms of dialect, and using patronymics, are, however, fast receding into the remote parts of the parish; and are only in use among the lower classes. Indeed, the latter custom (the use of patronymics) is quite extinct in the immediate vicinage of Bradford."

West Riding dialect literature seems to have started in south Yorkshire, around Sheffield and Barnsley, during the 1830s, when the cheap books of Yorkshire dialect verse from the North Riding probably began to encourage dialect writers living further south. Between 1830 and 1834 a number of dialect dialogue broadsheets called *The Sheffield Dialect: Be a Shevvild Chap* were in circulation and, like many dialect works, were published under a pseudonym. In 1836 the author revealed his true identity in the first number of *The Shevvild Chap's Annual* and signed himself Abel Bywater. This dialect annual had a twenty-year lifespan, having a profound effect on later dialect annuals and almanacs which were to follow.

Bywater's annual was the first of a long line of almanacs, which were the peculiar contribution to dialect writing by the dialect poets of the industrial West Riding. They had a wide appeal during their day. A very popular almanac like John Hartley's *Clock Almanac* topped the 75,000 copies per issue for many years. The West Riding almanacs were written largely in prose and contain the essence of Yorkshire wit at its best. Perhaps their greatest service to their contemporaries was to infuse a little lightness and philosophical humour into lives that must have been grim at the best of times. For us today, they are still humorous but dated. Perhaps their current interest lies in the exposition of a bygone society, the life and thoughts of the 19th century industrial communities for whom, and by members of whom, they were written.

The whole range of 19th century social history is to be found among their pages: the building of railroads and canals, the Poor Law, Chartist Movement, Co-operative Movement and Temperance reform, all find vocal expression in the almanacs. Professor Moorman, in the admirable introduction to his collection of Yorkshire dialect poetry published in 1915, sums up this remarkable development of West Riding dialect literature: "These almanacs furnish us with just such a mirror of 19th century industrial Yorkshire as the bound volumes of *Punch* furnish of the nation as a whole."

Anyone wishing to read more about these almanacs should consult Sir Ben Turner's and W. Hampson's paper published in The Yorkshire Dialect Society's *Transactions* for 1932, and Professor Moorman's introduction to his anthology. Stanley Ellis and the late Ben Dyson also produced a fine collection of almanac writings called *Yorkshire Pudding Olemnac,* published by the Yorkshire Dialect Society.

I will deal at length with what is perhaps the most famous of them all, John Hartley's *Clock Almanac*, but there were scores of dialect almanacs published in almost every West Riding town, and all of them followed the pattern laid down by Abel Bywater in his first almanac of 1836. They give us a very intimate picture of life in the steel cities, the textile towns and pit villages of Yorkshire 100 and more years ago.

Some are worth mentioning, for the names and the pseudonyms adopted by their authors reflect the humour their contents displayed. There was, for example, Tom Treddlehoyle's *Barnsla Foaks' Annual an' Pogmoor Olminack's*; Uriah Waketea's *'T' Bag o' Shoddy Olmenac* from Batley; and *'T' Coddy Miln Annual* by Peter Suteall. Dewsbury's almanac was *The Dewsbra Back o' t' Mooin Olmenac an' t' West Riding Historical Calendar* by Mungo Shoddy, B.MA. There was also an almanac from as far north as Pateley Bridge called *The Nidderdil Olminac* edited by Nattie Nidds frae Nidderdill.

Other well-known almanacs were published at Settle and Leeds, but the most famous and longest-running dialect magazine was John Hartley's Halifax almanac, *The Original Illuminated Clock Almenack*. Hartley edited it from 1867 until his death, when it was taken over by another very competent dialect-writer, Walter Hampson, who died in 1932. The almanac survived these editors and did not cease publication until 1957. It was originally founded in 1865 by Alfred Wilson, a hatter in Halifax, and the title and famous frontispiece illustration came from the illuminated clock on the front of Wilson's shop. John Hartley, who started life as a weaver, was in many ways the most versatile dialect-writer of his day, for he was at home in many forms of literary expression.

He was a good journalist, a first-class poet and a brilliant essayist in dialect, able to write on all sorts of subjects, from simple tales to abstract philosophical themes. He was essentially a humorist, though, and his humour ranged from broad geniality to pawky satire. He could begin an essay on "Fooils" ("Fools") with classical balance reminiscent of Malvolio's letter in *Twelfth Night*— "Ther's some born fooils, an' ther's some maks thersens fooils, an' ther's some gets made fooils on"—and he could pun at the expense of the standard language (and school board inspectors) as in *September Sports*:

"Aw heeard a bit sin abaat a schooil-inspector up i' Scammonden, who wor hearin' childer ther geography, 'What are the names of the principal English Lakes?' he axed. "Fooitball laikin, nur-and-spell laikin, pitch-an'-toss an' prize feightin' sed a lad abaat eight-year owd; an Aw dare bet a five-pahnd noat, if Aw hed one, 'at Yorkshire's th' only cahnty i' all England weer tha'd hey getten sich an answer."

Despite his works commanding a wide audience, John Hartley died a pauper in 1915 and was buried in a common grave out of his native county in Wallasey. He had led a very colourful life and visited North America for short stays twice during his lifetime. His collection of dialect essays, *Visits to America*, are masterly and give us a most interesting description in dialect of events ranging from a trip on an ice-breaker down the St. Lawrence in winter to what life was like in American cities just after the Civil War.

An innovation the almanac writers introduced into dialect writing was the use of extensive prose writing, generally in the form of the short story. Hartley excelled in the art of story-telling and capturing the character of the West Riding workers in his tales. He created two lovable characters called Sammywell Grimes and his wife, Mally, who were based on himself and his own wife. During his life he penned countless tales about this couple and recounted hundreds of humorous situations Sammywell got himself tangled up in.

Below is a typical piece of dialogue taken from Hartley's book, *Mally an' Me* (published in 1915), which was a collection of tales about Grimes and his wife from *The Clock Almanack*. Sammywell is being henpecked by his garrulous wife. He says barely a whole sentence throughout the entire tale, but we have a clear picture of his character, that of a typical West Riding "over-womaned" worker, and an even more vivid image of his wife, by the time she has finished her harangue:

If aw wor a Woman

"If aw wor a woman aw'd—"
"If tha wor a woman tha'd be a disgrace to ivveryboddy belangin to thi, an thart little else nah," sed Mally.
"Aw wor gooin to remark, at if aw wor a woman—"
"Eah! but tha ain't a woman, an if tha wor tha'd wish thisen a man agean, varry sharply. But if aw wor a man aw'd set a different example to what tha does. Aw wonder sometimes what tha'rt thinkin on, if tha ivver does think, which awm inclined to daat, unless its thinkin ha tha can contrive to be awkward and aggravatin."
"Well, but as aw wor gooin to say, If aw wor a—"
"Aw dooant want to hear owt tha has to say abaat it. A fine

woman tha'd mak! But aw wish tha wor foorced to swap places wi me for a wick. Aw should like to see ha tha'd fancy gettin up befoor dayleet ov a Monday mornin an start o' sich a weshin o' clooas as aw have to face ivvery wick; to say nowt abaat starchin an manglin an ironin. An then to start an brew a barrel o' ale for other fowk to sup; an then to bake—nivver to mention makkin th' beds an cleanin th' hearthstun, an' thi' meals to get ready, an' then to cleean th' haase throo top to bottom ivvery wick, an' darn th' stockins an put a claat here an a patch thear, an fifty moor things beside, an' nivver get a word o' thanks for it. Aw just wish tha wor a woman for an odd wick. Aw do, truly."

"As aw sed befoor, If aw wor a—"

"Aw'm capt tha hasn't moor sense nor to keep tawkin sich fooilishness. That knows tha ain't a woman an tha nivver can be—moor's th' pity. But if aw wor a man awd awther tawk sense or keep mi maath shut. Aw think sometimes at summat'll happen to thi as a judgment for hem sich an ungrateful tyke as tha art. Tha gets up in a mornin an finds thi braikfast ready, an if ther's owt i'th' haase at's nice an tasty tha gets it; and then tha walks aght, an comes to thi dinner, an off agean wol drinkin time, an after that tha awther gooas an caars i' some Jerryhoil, or else tha sits rockin thisen i'th' front o'th' foir, smookin thi' bacca an enjoyin thisen wol bedtime. Ther's some fowk dooant know when they're well done to. But aw know who it is at has to tew an slave all th' day, wi hardly a chonce to wipe th' sweat off mi face."

"But if tha'll lissen, aw wor gooin to remark, If aw wor—"

"Tha maks a deeal too monny remarks. Tha'll sit thear, remarkin an praichin bi th' haar together, an nivver give me a chonce to get in a word edgeways. But aw'm just sick an stall'd o' hearkenin to thi. Ther wor a time, years sin nah— but aw can remember it tho tha's forgetten it,—when tha used to sit an lissen to owt aw had to say, an my word wor law then. An if mi little finger warked tha'd hardly be able to sleep ov a neet for troublin abaat it. But it's different nah. Aw dooant believe it ud disturb thi if mi heead had to tummel off mi shoolders. Aw've studden a gooid deeal sin aw wor wed to thee, an aw expect aw'st ha to stand a lot moor; but one thing aw willn't put up wi, an that is, sittin an listenin to thee, an havin to keep mi tongue still. Soa tha knows."

"Well, but if aw wor—"

"Nah, let it stop just whear it is. Tha's getten a tawkin fit on aw know—aw wonder thi jaws dooan't wark. But aw willn't hear another word! Noa, net a word!"

"But if—"

"Ther's noa 'buts' abaat it! Hold thi noise, do! Tha'd tawk a hen an chickens to deeath. Tha wod. Aw wonder if aw shall ivver have a bit o' peace? Net befoor aw'm laid low, aw reckon."

aw'd—I'd; clooas—clothes; throo—from; claat—a large piece of cloth; awm capt—I'm surprised; nor—than; summat—something; wol—until; caars i' some Jerryhoil—settle down in some comfortable, out-of-the-way place; foir—fire; thisen—thyself; tew—tow, work hard; praichin—preaching; stall'd — out of patience; warked—ached; ud—would; tummel— tumble; studden—tolerated; aw'st ha—I shall have to.

Space will not permit the inclusion of other tales told in the hundreds of annuals and almanacs which proliferated during the 19th century throughout the industrial West Riding, but they form a formidable amount of literature—some of indifferent quality, some masterly—which was the staple reading material of the new population which sprung up and migrated into the West Riding towns and cities.

It is from the ranks of these prose dialect-writers that a later generation of Yorkshire writers, having the benefit of a wider and higher education, turned the standard tongue to good use to found the tradition of the Yorkshire novelist who has become a feature of 20th century English literature. The Hartleys and the Bywaters of the 19th century have been replaced by Priestley, Barstow, Storey, Waterhouse, Bentley and Braine of the 20th century to name but a few, all coming from the same industrial area and frequently writing about the same society, a hundred years on, that the early almanac writers were recording in their dialect works of the 19th century.

Before commenting further on the poetry in the West Riding during the mid-19th century, it may be as well to look at the North and East Riding writers who continued the tradition of dialect writing long established in their parts of the county.

John Castillo was not a Yorkshireman by birth, for he was born in Ireland in 1792, but his parents moved to England and settled in the North Riding at Lealboim Bridge when he was three years old. He became a stonemason by trade and joined the Wesleyan Methodist Movement in 1818, subsequently becoming famous locally as a preacher. Perhaps his most famous poem is *Awd Isaac*, probably printed first in 1831, but was included in several later collections of his poems. Castillo was a convert from Roman Catholicism to Methodism and his poetry reveals a strongly didactic and religious tone, which comes over effectively by reason of his simple and direct language. The four stanzas printed below, from *Awd Isaac*, demonstrates the directness of his style:

Awd Isaac

Oft hey Ah lang'd yon hill to clim,
To hey a bit mare prooase wi' him,
Wheas coonsel like a pleeasin dreeam,
    Is dear to me;

Sin' roond the warld sike men as he
    Seea few ther be.

Corrupted bukes he did detest,
For his wur ov the varry best;
This meead him wiser than the rest
    O' t'neeaburs roond,
Tho' poor i' purse, wi' senses blest,
    An' judgment soond.

Before the silvery neeght ov age,
The precepts ov the sacred page,
His meditation did engage,
    That race to run;
Like thooase, who 'spite o' Satan's age,
    The praaze bed won.

Bud noo his en's geean dim i' deeath,
Neea mare a pilgrim here on earth,
His sowl flits fra' her shell beneeath,
    To reealms o' day,
Whoor carpin care, an' pain, an' deeath,
    Are deean away.

prooase—discussion; *wheas*—whose; *sike*—such; *seea*—so; *neeght*—night; *een*—eyes; *geean*—gone; *mare*—more; *whoor*—where; *deean*—done.

George Newton Brown was another well-educated North Riding dialect-writer, who was a contemporary of the early West Riding writers. Brown was a lawyer by profession and is remembered for his best work, *The York Minster Screen* (reprinted by the Y.D.S.), which was first published in 1833. The poem concerns the damage done to the Minster Screen by a mad fire-raiser and the repairs made on it in 1832. The problems of altering the position of the screen are discussed with much racy humour by two North Riding farmers.

Florence Tweddell holds the distinction of being the first woman known to have used a Yorkshire dialect as her literary medium. She was born at Stokesley in 1824. Her husband, George Markham Tweddell, and she were master and matron of Bury Industrial and Ragged Schools for some years. She died in 1899; her *Rhymes and Sketches* to illustrate the Cleveland Dialect were published by her husband in 1875. Her poem, *Coom, stop at yam to-neet, Bob*, has a theme the West Riding poets often wrote about; drunkenness in a poverty stricken home. It was a vice loudly condemned by Victorian society and more prevalent in the towns than the country. It marks a departure by a North Riding poet from the traditional rural topics.

Coom, Stop at Yam to-neet, Bob

"Coom, stop at yam to-neet, Bob,
    Dean't gan oot onnywbere:
Thoo gets thisel t' leeast vex'd, lad,
    When thou sits i' t' awd airm-chair.

"There's Keat an' Dick beath want thee
    to stop an' tell a teale:
Tak little Keatie o' thy knee,
    An' Dick'll sit on t' steal.

"Let's have a happy neet, Bob,
    Tell all t' teales thoo can tell;
For givin' pleasure to the bairns
    Will dea thee good thisel.

"I knaw it's sea wi' me, Bob,
    For oft when I've been sad,
I've laik'd an' laugh'd wi' them, mon,
    Untel my heart 's felt glad.

"An' sing that laatle sang, Bob,
    Thoo used to sing to me,
When oft we sat at t' river saade,
    Under t' awd willow tree.

"What happy taames them was, Bob,
    Thoo niver left me then
To gan to t' yal-hoose neet be neet
    Amang all t' drunken men.

"I does my best for thoo, Bob,
    An' thoo sud dea t' seame for me:
Just think what things thoo promised me
    Asaade t' awd willow tree!"

"I prithee say na mair, lass,
    I see I ain't dean reet;
I'll think of all thoo's said to me,
    An' stop at yam to-neet.

"I'll try to lead a better life—
    I *will*, an' that thoo'll see!
Fra this taame fo'th I'll spend my neets,
    At yam, wi' t' bairns an' thee!"

yam—home; *gan oot*—go out; *thisel*—thyself; *steal*—stool; *bairns*—children; *laik'd*—played; *taames*—times; *yal-hoose*—ale-house.

Professor Moorman, in his collection of Yorkshire dialect poetry in 1915, draws attention to the fact that the Western Dales were less fruitful in the production of dialect poetry during the 19th century than other parts of the county. The same situation is still true today. The Yorkshire Dialect Society found it difficult recently to amass enough poems from the Western Dales to compile a new anthology. Wensleydale has produced more active interest in verse than other dales, and Kit Calvert has written some good material in the Hawes dialect in recent years; nevertheless, compared with the rest of Yorkshire, little material has come out of the upper reaches of the Yorkshire Dales since Tom Twistleton, the Settle farmer, produced his *Poems in the Craven Dialect* in 1869.

Lower down Craven, James Henry Dixon, though born in London in 1803, was brought up in Skipton and lived in Grassington for a time. He was more famous as an antiquarian and collector of dialect poems than as a writer, but he did pen a few dialect poems himself, and in a long poem called *Slaadburn Faar*, published in 1871, five years before his death, he gives a humorous account of a Grassington farmer and his wife riding to Slaidburn to attend the local fair.

Thomas Blackah (1828-95) was a lead-miner who lived at Pateley Bridge and edited the Nidderdale almanac mentioned earlier under the pseudonym "Nattie Nidds." In 1867 he had published a collection of his own verse called *Songs and Poems in the Nidderdale Dialect*, which make entertaining reading. One poem in particular, *Pateley Reeaces*, has some vivid details of Wharfedale worthies, as the following two stanzas show:

> "Fat Sal fra t' Knott scarce gat ta t' spot,
> Afore sha lost her bustle,
> Which sad mishap quite spoiled her shap,
> An' meeade her itch an' hustle.

Lile pug-nooas'd Nell, fra Kettlewell,
Com in her Dolly Vardin,
All frill'd and starch'd sha proodly march'd
Wi' squintin' Jooa fra Bardin."

shap—shape; lile—little; Dolly Vardin—short, bunched-up—overskirt.

John Thwaite (1873-1941) also came from the upper dale country, being born near Aysgarth. He was living at Hawes when he died. His poetry will be remembered most for the sensitive feeling he had for his native countryside and the natural life found in it. A posthumous collection of his verse, *Wensleydale Dialect Rhymes* was published by Dalesman Publishing Co. in 1946. The opening stanza of his poem *To a Dipper* reveals his keen eye for detail and his love of nature:

"Thi bonny briest's as white as sna',
It's pure, ay, lily pure;
An' puts i' t' shade them ban's o' foam
'At sails away doon Eure."

By the mid-19th century dialect-writing was firmly established as a popular, and, for the publishers, very lucrative pastime. Dialect literature was widely read and by 1915 works like *The Clock Almanack* were averaging annual sales of 120,000 each edition. William Wright, better known locally in Keighley as Bill o' th' Hoylus End, sold over 100,000 copies of his *History o' th' Haworth Railway* when it first came out in the 1870s and it sold many reprints afterwards. In some ways the mid-19th and late-19th century produced the most impressive examples of West Riding dialect verse, each community having its dialect poet. For example, between Bradford and Keighley, a matter of only ten miles, there were five well-defined communities served by their own poets each writing prolifically, starting with Ben Preston, Edmund Hatton, Abraham Holdroyd and William Cudworth all of Bradford, James Burnley of Shipley, James Waddington of Saltaire, John Nicholson of Bingley and William Wright of Keighley.

The themes of these West Riding writers fall roughly into two main groups, those connected with the industrial, domestic and working conditions in the towns and those sentimentalising country life as an idyllic life far removed from the miserable conditions many of the townsfolk had to live and work in. John Hartley's and Ben Preston's poetry capture the poverty and hunger of the 1840s and, although their verse now seems grossly sentimental (like the novels of Dickens), it is well for a modern reader to remember the miserable conditions which formed the background of their verse, and with which the poets themselves were often familiar. Pauper boys grubbing about in Halifax streets for rotten food and Bradford weavers too impoverished to contemplate a marriage which would inflict suffering on a sweetheart seem over-exaggerated subjects to a modern reader, but they were real enough features of 19th century West Riding life, as the following poems by Ben Preston and John Hartley show:

I niver can call her mi wife by Ben Preston

I'm a weyver, ye knaw, an' awf deead,
  So I do all at iver I can
To put away aat o' my heead
  The thowts an' the aims of a man.
Eight shillin' i' t'wick's what I am,
  When I've varry gooid wark an' full time,
An' I think it's a sorry consarn
     For a fella at's just in his prime.

Bud aar maister says things is as weel
   As they have been or iver can be,
An' I happen sud think so misel
   If he'd nobbud swop places we' me.
Bud he's welcome to all he can get,
   I begrudge him o' noan of his brass,
An' I'm nowt bud a madlin to fret,
   Or to think o' yon beautiful lass.

I niver can call her mi wife,
 My love I sal niver mak knawn,
Yit the sorra that darkens her life
 Thraws its shadda across o' my awn.
When I knaw at her heart is at eease,
 Theer is sunshine an' singin' i' mine;
An' misfortunes may come as they pleease,
 Yit they seldom can mak me repine.

Bud that Chartist wor nowt bud a slope—
   I were fooild by his speeches an' rhymes,
For his promises wattered my hope,
   An' I leng'd for his sunshiny times;
Bud I feel at my dearest desire
   Within me'll wither away;
Like an ivy stem trailin' i' t' mire,
   It's deein' for t' want of a stay.

When I laid i' my bed day an' neet,
   An' were geen up by t' doctors for deead,
God bless her! Shoo'd coom wi' a leet
   An' a basin o' grewil an' breead.
An' I once thowt I'd ant wi' it all,
   Bud so kindly shoo chatted an' smiled,

I were fain to turn ovver to t' wall,
    An' to bluther an' roar like a child.

An' I said, as I thowt of her een,
    Each breeter for t' tear at were in 't,
It's a sin to be niver forgeen,
  To yoke her to famine an' stint;
So I'll e'en travel forrad throo life,
  Like a man throo a desert unknawn;
I mun ne'er have a home nor a wife,
  Bud my sorras'll all be my awn.

So I trudge on alone as I owt,
    An' whativer my troubles may be,
They'll be sweetened, poor lass, wi' the thowt
    At I've niver browt trouble to thee.
Yit a bird has its young uns to guard,
    A wild beast a mate in his den,
An' I cannot bud think at it's hard—
    Nay, deng it, I'm roarin' agen!

maister—master, mill-owner; madlin—fool; slope—fraud; wattered—watered, encouraged; deem—dying; shoo'd—she would; leet—light; grewil—gruel; bluther an' roar—weep and wail.

Bite Bigger by John Hartley

As I hurried through t' taan to my wark,
    —I were lat, for all t' buzzers had gooan—
I happen'd to hear a remark
    At 'ud fotch tears thro th' heart of a stooan.
It were rainin', an' snawin', an' cowd,
    An' t' flagstones were cover'd wi' muck,

An' th' east wind both whistled an' howl'd,
    It saanded like nowt bud ill luck.
When two little lads, donn'd i' rags,
    Baat stockin's or shoes o' their feet,
Com trapsin, away ower t' flags,
    Boath on 'em sodden'd wi' t' weet.
Th' owdest mud happen be ten,
    T' young un be haulf on't, no more;
As I look'd on, I said to misen,
    "God help fowks this weather at's poor!"
T' big un samm'd summat off t' graand,
    An' I look'd just to see what 't could be,
'T were a few wizen'd flaars he'd faand,
    An' they seem'd to hae fill'd him wi' glee.
An' he said, "Coom on, Billy, may be
    We sal find summat else by an' by;
An' if not, tha mun share these wi' me,
    When we get to some spot wheer it's dry."
Light-hearted, they trotted away,
    An' I follow'd, 'cause t' were i' my rooad;
But I thowt I'd ne'er seen sich a day,
    It weren't fit to be aat for a tooad.
Sooin t' big un agean slipp'd away,
    An' samm'd summat else aat o' t' muck;
An' he cried aat, "Look here, Bill, to-day
    Ain't we blest we' a seet o' gooid luck?
"Here's a apple, an' t' mooast on it's saand,
    What's rotten I'll throw in t' street.
Wern't it gooid to lig theer to be faand?
    Naa boath on us can have a treat."
So he wip'd it an' rubb'd it, an' then
    Said, "Billy, thee bite off a bit;
If tha hasn't been lucky thisen,
    Tha sal share wi' me sich as I get."

So t' little un bate off a touch,
  T' other's face beam'd wi' pleasure all through,
An' he said, "Nay, tha hasn't taen mich,
  Bite agean, an' bite bigger, naa do."
I waited to hear nowt no more;
  Thinks I, there's a lesson for me;
Tha's a heart i' thy breast, if tha'rt poor;
    T' world were richer wi' more sich as thee.
Two pence were all t' brass at I had,
  An' I meant it for ale when com nooin;
But I thowt, I'll go give it yon lad,
  He desarves it for what he's been doin'.
So I said, "Lad, here's twopence for thee,
  For thisen." An' they star'd like two geese;
Bud he said, whol t' tear stood in his ee,
  "Naa, it'll just be a penny apiece."
"God bless thee! Do just as tha will,
  An' may better days speedily come;
Though clamm'd an' hauf donn'd, my lad, still
    Tha'rt a deal nearer Heaven nor some."

lat—late; buzzers—mill buzzers summoning workers to the mills; flagstones—pavement; donn'd—dressed; baat—without; misen—myself; at's—that's; samm'd—picked up; flaars —flowers; mun—must; jig—lie down; brass—money; clamm 'd—starved; hauf—half; nor—than.

Other poems like William Cudworth's *A Hearthstone Gem*, Hartley's *Aght o' Wark*, and Prof. Moorman's *A Dalesman's Litany* capture the bitterness and misery that the effects of the Industrial Revolution inflicted on the operatives. Professor F. W. Moorman's poem is quite unique in its way for Moornian was not a Yorkshireman. He was born at Ashburton in Devon, but when he came north as Professor of English Language at Leeds University he made a special study of Yorkshire dialects, and so immersed himself in them that he himself became a very proficient writer of dialect verse. He was a profound scholar and did much to promote dialect study and evaluate the literary worth of dialect literature before his tragic death in 1919. His *A Dalesman's Litany* captures all the horrors that a Victorian dales farm labourer had to undergo in West Riding towns, when he was forced to find work in them after being expelled from his rented cottage in the country.

A Dalesman's Litany

It's hard when fowks can't find their wark
    Wheer they've bin bred an' born;
When I were young I awlus thowt
    I'd bide 'mong t' roots an' corn.
But I've bin forced to work i' towns,
    So here's my litany:
Frae Hull, an' Halifax, an' Hell,
    Gooid Lord, deliver me!

When I were courtin' Mary Ann,
    T'owd squire he says one day:
'I've got no bield for wedded fowks;
    Choose wilt ta wed or stay?'
I couldn't gie up t' lass I loved,
    To t' town we had to flee:
Frae Hull, an' Halifax, an' Hell,
    Gooid Lord, deliver me!

I've wrowt i' Leeds an' Hudthersfel',
    An' addled honest brass;
I' Bradforth, Keighley, Rotherham,
    I've kept my barns an' lass.
I've travelled all three Ridin's round,

And once I went to sea:
Frae forges, mills, an' coalin' boats,
   Gooid Lord, deliver me!

I've walked at neet through Sheffield loans,
   'T were t' same as bein' i' Hell;
Furnaces thrast out tongues o' fire,
   An' roared like t' wind on t' fell.
I've sammed up coals i' Barnsley pits,
   Wi' muck up to my knee:
Frae Sheffield, Barnsley, Rotherham,
   Gooid Lord, deliver me!

I've seen grey fog creep ower Leeds Brig
   As thick as bastile soup;
I've lived wheer fowks were stowed away
   Like rabbits in a coop.
I've watched snow float down Bradforth Beck
   As black as ebiny:
Frae Hunslet, Holbeck, Wibsey Slack,
   Gooid Lord, deliver me!

But now, when all wer childer's fligged,
   To t' coontry we've coom back.
There's fotty mile o' heathery moor
   Twix' us an' t' coal-pit slack.
An' when I sit ower t' fire at neet,
   I laugh an' shout wi' glee:
Frae Bradforth, Leeds, an' Huthersfel',
Frae Hull, an' Halifax, an' Hell,
   T' gooid Lord's delivered me!

bield—shelter; *wrowt*—worked; *addled*—earned; *barns*—children; *loans*—lanes; *sammed up*—picked up; *bastile soup*

—*workhouse soup; childer—children; fligged—flown away; slack—powdery coal-dust.*

There is an interesting feature about these depressing dialect poems of the 19th century—they all end up on an optimistic note, more often than not in a rather sentimentalised religious vein. The oppressiveness of life seemed to bring out the West Riding worker's inborn humour, which made him laugh in fate's face. William Wright, of Keighley, wrote a delightful poem along just this theme, exhorting his fellow men not to let life get them down. It is called *Come, nivver dee i' thi shell*; never be defeated by backing down from life.

"Come, Nivver Dee i' Thi Shell"
by William Wright (1836-97)

"Come, nivver dee i' thi shell, owd lad,"
Are words but rudely said;
Though they may cheer some stricken heart,
Or raise some wretched head;
For they are words I love mysel,
They're music to my ear;
They muster up fresh energy
An' chase each doubt an' fear.
Nivver dee i' thi shell, owd lad,
Though tha be poor indeed;
Ner lippen ta long i' th' turnin' up
Sa mich ov a friend in need;
Fur few ther are, an' far between,
That help a poor man thru;
An' God helps them at help therseln,
An' they hey friends enew.

Nivver dee i' thi shell, owd lad,
Whativver thi creditors say;
Tell um at least tha'rt foarst ta owe,
If tha artant able ta pay;
An' if they nail thi bits o' traps,
An' sell thi dish an' spooin;
Remember fickle forten lad,
Shoo changes like the mooin.

Nivver dee i' thi shell, owd lad,
Though some may laugh an' scorn;
There wor nivver a neet afore ta neet,
Bud what ther' com a morn;
An' if blind forten used tha bad,
Sho's happen noan so meean;
Ta morn al come, an' then fer some
The sun will shine ageean.

Nivver dee i' thi shell, owd lad,
Bud let thi motto be,—
"Onward!" an' "Excelsior;"
An' try for t' top o' t' tree:
An' if thi enemies still pursue,
Which ten-ta-one they will,
Show um owd lad, tha'rt doin' weel,
An' climin' up the hill.

lippen—delay; enew—enough; artant—are not; if they nail thi bits o' traps—if the bailiffs take away your few possessions; spooin—spoon.

The 19th century poets in all three Ridings composed many humorous poems and some of the better ones have a strong satirical vein running through them. Victorian establishment, in the form of pedantic schoolmasters and prudish parsons, is frequently the target for the dialect writers' scorn. George Lancaster, an East Riding poet born in 1846, and John Hartley, penned several satirical poems but the following two will suffice to show just how the Victorian schoolmaster and the Victorian parson were taken down a peg or two gently but firmly.

A Yorkshire Farmer's Address to a Schoolmaster
by George Lancaster

Good day to you, Mister skealmaisther, the evenin' is
    desperate fine,
I thowt I wad gie ye a call aboot that young sonnie o'
    mine.
I couldn't persuade him to come, sea I left him behont
    me at yam,
Bud somehoo it's waintly possess'd me to mak a
    skealmaisther o' Sam.
He's a kind of slack-back, I knaw, I niver could get him
    to work,
He scarcelins wad addle his saut wiv a ploo, or a shovel,
    or fork.
I've tried him agean an' agean, but I finnd that he's nea
    use at yam,
Sea me an' my missus agreed to mak a skealmaisther o'
    Sam.
If I send him to wark, why, he'll chunther an' gie me
    the awfullest leaks,
He'd deal rayther lig upo'd sofy wi' novels an' them
    soort o' beaks.
Sea I tbowt a skealmaisther wad suit him, a lowse soort
    o' job, do ye see,
Just to keep a few bairns oot o' mischief, as easy as easy
    can be.

Of coorse, you've to larn 'em to coont, an' to figure a
    bit, an' to read,
An' to sharpen 'em up if they're numskulls, wiv a
    lalldabber ower their heead,
Bud it's as easy as easy, ye knaw, an' I think it wad just
    suit orr Sam,
An' my missus, she's just o' my mind, for she says that
    he's nea use at yam.
It was nobbut this mornin' I sent him to gan an' to
    harrow some land;
He was boamin asleep upo' d' fauf, wiv a rubbishly
    beak iv his hand;
I gay him a bunch wi' my feat, an' rattled him yarmin'
    off yam.
Sea I think that I'll send him to you, you mun mak a
    skealmaisther o' Sam.
He's still an' a runty young fellow, I think that he'll
    grow up a whopper,
He'd wallop the best lad you've got, an' I think he wad
    wallop him proper;
Bud still he's a slack-back, ye knaw, an' seem' he's nea
    use at yam,
I think I shall send him to you, you mun mak a skeal-
    maisther o' Sam.

behont—behind; yam—home; vaintly—strangely; slack-back —idle person; saut—salt, i.e. keep; ploo—plough; chunther —grumble; leaks—looks; hg—lie; lowse—easy-going; lalldabber—cuff; boamin—trailing along; fauf—fallow; bunch — kick; yarmin—yelping; runty—thick-set.

Ahr Mary's Bonnet by John Hartley

Hey ye seen ahr Mary's bonnet?
It's a stunner an' noa mistak,
Ther's a bunch o' roases on it,
An' a feather dahn her back,
Yeller ribbon, an' fine laces,
An' a cock-o-doodle doo,
An' arahnd her bonny face,
Is a string o' posies, blue.
When shoo went ta chu'ch last Sunda,
Parson couldn't finnd his text,
An' fat owd Mrs. Grundy said,
"Ah, Mary, pray what next?"
T'lads winked at one another,
T'lasses sniggered i' ther glee,
An' th' whooal o' t' congregation
Hed her bonnet i' ther ee.
Then t' choir started singin',
An' the first hymn they sang,
Wer all abaht the flahers,
Of fifty summers gone.
An' when they saw ahr Mary,
They made a mullock on it.
For they thowt 'at all them flahers,
Hed bin put on Mary's bonnet.
Then t'parson said most kindly,
Ther wer non offence intended,
That flaher shows wer aht o'place,
In chu'ch wheer saints attended;
An' if his errin' sister,
Wished ta find her way to glory,
Shoo shouldn't carry on her head,
A whoal conservatory.

> Nah ahr Mary isn't short o' pluck,
> Shoo jumped up in a minnit,
> Shoo lewked es if sha'd swallered t' chu'ch,
> An' ivverybory in it.
> "Parson," shoo said, "yer head is bare,
> Nowt in it, an' nowt on it,
> Suppose yer put some flahers theer,
> Like these 'at's on my bonnet."

mullock—complete hash.

The Yorkshire Dialect Society was founded in 1897 and has been instrumental throughout its distinguished history collecting, collating and encouraging research into not only those dialects native to Yorkshire, but also many dialects throughout England. It has also uncovered a mass of infor- mation about Yorkshire folklore, customs and place-names which otherwise would have been lost. Not least among the benefits it has given Yorkshire dialect-lovers has been the means for dialect-writers to find an outlet for their verse and prose through its two annual publications, the *Transactions* (since 1898) and the *Summer Bulletin* (since 1954).

The Yorkshire Dialect Society was founded when the English Dialect Society ceased to exist. It began in the West Riding with that typical independent streak Yorkshiremen possess when they wish to preserve something worthwhile. A Yorkshire scholar, Professor Joseph Wright, of Oxford University, was compiling a mammoth dictionary, *The English Dialect Dictionary* and the Yorkshire Dialect Society was formed to aid him in that great work as well as preserving Yorkshire's traditional dialects.

The first President of the Y.D.S. was the Marquis of Ripon and among the first list of members are some very notable names in scholarship at both local and national levels, names like Professor Joseph Wright, Walter Skeat, Charles Federer and Henry Bradley. Yorkshire antiquarians like Harry Speight, J. Horsfall Turner and Canon Atkinson were founder members as were the dialect poets John Hartley, Ben Preston, W. Fowler, Tom Twistleton and the novelist J. Keighley Snowden. The name of Dr. Wilfrid J. Halliday, appears in a membership list for 1915, and from that day to this, distinguished men and women of English letters have been members of the Y.D.S. Yorkshire folk from all walks of life have contributed to the study and development of Yorkshire dialects and their literature.

In his inaugural address of 1898 the Marquis of Ripon said: "Why should we make a study of those dialects which we admit are departing? The answer is very simple—because they are closely connected with the history of our country and the history of our language. The study of the ancient languages of any country is of the highest value in understanding the national history and the national character."

A reservation I would make about the Marquis of Ripon's statement is that our dialects are not departing. They are changing, rapidly perhaps in the present century, but they have always changed. As long as people are different, as long as they live different types of life in different social groups, they will speak differently even within national boundaries. Dialects are the local differences of speech, which define social groups one from another at many levels of life.

One great change that has taken place in dialect literature, especially in the West Riding, is that dialect has become the literary medium of a wider range of people. Writers with the highest education, as well as people who have spoken dialect as their only means of linguistic expression, write good dialect verse and prose. Dales shepherds, textile workers, foundry men, teachers, accountants, farmers, housewives, physicians, soldiers—even cabinet ministers—have turned to their native Yorkshire dialects since the turn of the century when they wished to write poetry or prose. In the last century Emily Bronte used Yorkshire dialect widely in her classic *Wuthering Heights*; as did her sister Charlotte in "*Shirley*." In the 20th century J. B. Priestley created a lovable Brudderfordian character, Jess Oakroyd, in *The Good Companions*. George Bernard Shaw also gave St. Joan the characteristics of a West Riding dialect speaker based upon his readings of Yorkshire dialect literature supplied him by his friend, Sir Ben Turner. G.B.S. also based the character of Henry Higgins in *Pygmalion* on Henry Sweet, the great linguist who was an early member of the Y.D.S.

Dialect writing has long had a place in the county's news- papers and journals, which have played a part in stimulating original and worthwhile writing. In the 1960s the Y.D.S. collected the verse of 20th century and more recent dialect-writers and published it in three anthologies corresponding to the dialects of the three Ridings. An interesting feature about these anthologies is the number of women dialect writers contributing to the collections. In the *Cleveland Anthology*, covering the North Riding, Brenda English, Irene Sutcliffe, Ruth Hedger, Muriel Carr and Mary Reed are prominent. The East Riding anthology has Clare Ellin, Kathleen Stark, Florence Hopper, Elsie Grassby and Mrs. F. E. Jackson among its writers. And the West Riding women writers are Gwen Wade, Marion Pobjoy, Ellen P. Merunowicz, Ethel Walter, Emma O'Connel, Winifred Littlewood, Elsie Clare, and Mary Thackeray Waller. The late Dorothy Una Ratcliffe tried her hand at all three dialects, and an increasing number of women writers have had their verse and prose published in various numbers of *Summer Bulletin* and *Transactions* over the past 20 years.

In *A Cleveland Anthology* Ruth Hedger displays a fine ability to combine humour with detail in a description of a North Riding country churchyard in *Sheeap i t' Chotchyard*, whose punch-line is retained till the very end.

Sheeap i t' Chotchyard

Awd Mister Fuzzock war sleepin' soond,
Safe under t'groond,
Till summat meead im to'n iv is beddin.—
Sitha, a weddin!
Bud thing at put im i sike a steeat
War t'chotchyard geeat;
It was fassen'd back, as Billy'd putten it,
An neeabody'd shutten it!
T'sheeap gat in—they did, Ah seear—
They meeastlins deea.
A weddin prawcession they ed, an seean
Damage war deean.
All ovver t'graves they spreead, nivver stoppin;
An seean war croppin,
Champin an chavellin ollin an' berry—
By, they war merry!
Wi Kessmas wreeaths for a weddin feeast,
Biggest ti t'leeast.
"Bon!" sez awd Fuzzock tiv Arthur Hall,
"This fair caps all!
Ah can feeal em stampin like elephants;
An all t'chrysanths
At Mary Ann ed putten atop,
Nut yan 'll stop!"
"Aye," sez Arthur, "an Jane's good wreeath,
They's getten beeath!

Ah awps they'll suffer for this day's lark
Wi belly-wark.
Cud Ah nobbut get oot, Ah'd flay yon Billy
Whahl e went silly—
Leeavin yon geeat an spoilin oor sleeap!
Ah tented sheeap
On Gooadland Greean when Ah war a lad,
An if mah Dad
Ed cotched ma leeavin t'yat unsnecked,
Ah'd nut ev recked
Varry mich ti mi supper at neet,
Nor mi breeaks-seeat!
Bud fawks nooadays is a poorish lot;
We've getten t'best spot."
"Aye," sez Fuzzock, "it's t'trewth thoo's saying...
Theer's t'organ playin;
An t'neeam o' yon bonny piece sha plays
Caps t'lot—it's bloody *Sheeap May Safely Graze!"*

groond—ground; beddin—grave; sitha—look!; sike—such; geeat—gate; seear—sure; meeastlins deea—usually do; ollin —holly; Kessmas—Christmas; bell y-wark—stomach ache; whahl—until; tented—watched; t' yat unsnecked—the gate unlocked; recked—reckoned; breeaks-seat—breeches-bottom.

A Cleveland Anthology was the first collection of verse composed in the Cleveland area of North Yorkshire to be published since 1877, and its editor, the late Bill Cowley, presents a fine historical survey of dialect-writing in North Yorkshire from the earliest writing done there to the present. He has an interesting comment to make on an important difference between modern North Riding dialect and the modern dialects of the industrial West Riding; he points out the effects that the comparative lack of industrialisation in North Yorkshire has had on the native dialects:

"Partly because of this (lack of industry), our dialect has remained fairly static, linked with farming (or fishing) and with the older ways of farming. In the West Riding, dialect is the language of everyone. It is flexible. It can be used in the modern idiom (as F. A. Carter and Fred Brown use it). This cannot be done with Cleveland dialect, a forgotten language now to the majority of Cleveland's inhabitants. It just doesn't go with the combine-harvester, grain-drier and tractor-mounted plough! Near the hills the younger generation can still speak it, with a limited vocabulary. Ten miles away on the plain it is already one generation and, on Tees- side, two generations away."

It is an invidious task selecting material from these three current anthologies of Yorkshire dialect, but from the North Riding selection I chose one poem by the late Stanley Umpleby, a former secretary of the Yorkshire Dialect Society and co-editor with Dr. Halliday of *White Rose Garland*, the most comprehensive collection of and commentary on Yorkshire dialect writings published to date. A. S. Umpleby was a dialect poet who worked hard at his verse, constantly experimenting with it and adapting it to fit classical English verse-forms such as the ballade and rondeau. His *Ballade of Staithes*, reproduced below, shows the high standard to which he raised his level of dialect verse, achieved conscientiously and earnestly over many years.

Ballade of Staithes

Ah like ti gan ti Steeas i spring,
That's t'tahm sha allus leeaks er best;
When t'mizzle-thrush an blackis sing,
An t'cuddy bigs er lahl roond nest:
When t'scented breeze blaws oot o' t'west,
An t'primrooases leeaks up to t'shooer,

When Awkness trees wi blossom's drissed,
An t'silverwhips is oot i flooer.

Let me be theer when t'childer bring
Ther flooers fre t'Yak-Riggs, threy abreeast;
Milkmaids an daisies iv a string—
Ye deean't knaw which is t'bonniest:
An welcome's theer for onny guest,
Neea matters whether rich or poor:
Ah allus gan aboot bein press'd
When t'silverwhips is oot i flooer.

Whahl o' t'awd rocks yon flithers cling,
Whahl Steeas craft rayds ower t'ocean crest,
Whalil t'pets is all aboot o t'wing,
An sea-wrack up o t'sand is kesst,
Awd Steens 'll stand tiv onny test:
Wi cliffs, rocks, woods, bods, flooers an moor:
    Bud gi me er—why noo ye've guess'd—
When t'silverwhips is oot i flooer.

Envoy

Missis, awaya! Wail ev a rist,
Wheer ther's real life at onny oor;
Wheer awd an young sing, laugh an jest,
An t'silverwhips is oot i flooer.

With very slight variations, the dialects of the East Riding are similar to those of the north. The subjects for the dialect literature of the East and North Ridings are identical, too, and are centred around agricultural life and the sea life of the coastal communities. There are, however, distinct differences apparent in the approach of East and North Riding writers to their themes, for the agricultural hierarchy, like the farms, in the East Riding was larger and more complex than the smaller farms further north, especially those on the North Yorkshire moors.

Bill Cowley is also the editor of *An East Yorkshire Anthology* and he was an apt choice to edit the collection, for he himself was a competent dialect poet, as well as being a farmer, and was well able to point out the differences which exist between the East and North Riding dialects, differences which are not always apparent at times to West Riding ears like my own. His introduction to *An East Riding Anthology*, like his earlier editing of *A Cleveland Anthology*, also contains a first-rate historical survey of the region.

The most poignant poems in the collection are those about the 1914-18 war. These war poems are a special feature of his anthology for no war poetry appears in the anthologies of verse from the North and West Ridings. I find it a surprising feature of West Riding dialect verse that, as far as I know, no poems were written about the 1914-18 war when the casualties suffered by West Riding regiments were appalling. Whole battalions were wiped out several times during that war. (For example, the Leeds Pals Battalion of the West Yorkshire Regiment lost 823 men killed in one day at the opening of the Somme offensive on July 1st, 1916, and the battalion was subsequently re-formed several times.) A. Irving Parke's and Quentin Nicholas's two poems capture the pathos and wastefulness of war in much the same way Wilfred Owen's verses express the pity of war in the standard language.

Oor Bit (1916) by A. Irving Parke

T'sun we shahnin breet ower t'ling,
An t'bods ed nowt ti deea bud sing;
For all t'Wold shooted "Lang live t'King!"
    When oor lad went ti t'War.

T'staggath wer filled an all theaked doon,
T'breckon an t'ling tonned ask an broon,
An t'awd cat snuggled close ti t'yoon,
    When oor lad fowt i t'War.

Corn wer threshed, nowt left bud streea,
An t'awd man set wi nowt ti deea
For ice an snaw ligged ivvrywheer,
    When oor lad deed i t'War.

bods—birds; bud—but; staggath—stack yard; theaked doon—thatched down; breckon—bracken; ask an broon—dry and brown; yoon—oven; streea—straw; ligged—lay.

Roll of Honour by Quentin Nicholas

When, of a Sunda, Ah sits i mi pew,
    Ah sees a list o lads at yance Ah knew,
An then it ardlins seems a day sin last
Ah spooak tiv em, though monny years as passed.
There's Dick at war a champion wi t'ploo,
    Ti set a rig an furrow straight an true,
An Ben at snickled monny a fine fat hare,
    E'll nivver trouble t'keepers onny mair!
Arry, that oor Sarah used to cooart,
    An Bob at war a dab at ivvery spooart.
When Ah war young, Ah palled on wiv em all,
    Bud noo they're nobbut neeanis upon t'choch wall.

yance—once; *ardlins*—hardly; *tiv*—to; *ploo*—plough; *rig*—ridge; *snickled*—poached; *war a dab*—was an expert; *neeams*—names; *choch*—church.

The anthology for the East Riding is dedicated to the memory of the late F. Austin Hyde, for many years a member of the Y.D.S. Council and, with his sister, Muriel Carr, a prolific dialect-writer and scholar until his death in 1965. A novel feature of Austin Hyde's dialect writing was his ability to write dialect plays, which became a feature of 20th century Yorkshire dialect literature in all three Ridings. (F. A. Carter and James Gregson are two West Riding exponents of dialect drama, and Dorothy Una Ratcliffe also wrote some good one-act plays which have been widely acclaimed.) Perhaps the best known of Austin Hyde's poems is *Depper, Awd Mare*, a poem written on a traditional Yorkshire dialect theme, especially in the East Riding where the horse held a place of great significance on the land before the coming of mechanised farming and tractors.

Depper, Awd Mare

Hev I ony awd osses young fellow frey Ull?
Thoo's willin tae buy em? Gie value i full?
Why yis, I ha'e yan, i this paddock doon here,
Cohup, then! Coom on, then! Coom, Depper awd meer!
No, she dizn't coom gallopin, bud then, you see,
A mare's a bit wankle-like, tonned twenty-three.
Thoo'll mebbe not be quite sae frisky thisen
When thoo's seen thi great grandsons grow up to be men!
Weel, what will I tak for her? Why noo, she's fat,
An' they tell me you give a bit extra far that,
Bud I might as well tell tha, thoo'll not buy that meer
If thoo stands there an bids me fra noo tae next year!
She was t'fost foal I ad when I corn upo'd place

An fost she's been allus, i shaft, pole or thrace.
She's ploughed, drilled an harrowed, rolled, scruffled an led,
An mothered Beaut, Boxer, Prince, Cobby an Ned.
If threshin-machine gat stuck fast on its way
Young osses wad plunge, rahve an tew hauf o'd day,
Bud afoor it gat shifted, it allus was "Here,
Away thoo gans, Thoddy, an fetch us t'owd meer!"
When stacks was a fire, afoor motor-car days,
She galloped tae Driffield when t'spot was ablaze,
Ower field, ditch an hedgerow for t'gainest way doon,
Saved buildings, an hoos an three pikes, I'll be boon!
When t'missus was badly, when t'baby was born,
'Twas a life an death jonny for t'doctor that morn.
An though she'd been workin at plough all day lang
T'meer galloped as tho she knew summat was wrang.
Wi never a whip, nor a jerk on her rein
She went like a whirlwind an com hack again
Wi t'doctor an nuss, just i time tae save life—
Aye, Depper, I owe thoo baith dowter an wife.
On friends at's sae faithful we doan't turn wer backs,
Nor send em for slaughter tae d'foreigner's axe,
Nor let em be worked tae their death across t'sea,
Wheer niver a Yorkshire voice shouts "Wahve!" nor "Gee!"
No, noo at she's neither young, bonny nor sound,
She awns t'lahtle paddock, it's pensioner's ground,
An stall i yon stable, hay, beddin an corn,
I reckon she's addled a spot of her awn!
An when yon day comes at we do ha'e tae pairt,
She'll gan in a way at'll not brek her hairt,
An t'land at she's worked on an loved twenty year
At last'll lig leet on my faithful awd meer!

frey—from; awd meer—old mare; wankle like—stiff and unsteady; tonned—turned; thisen—yourself; corn up 'd—took over; thrace—traces; rahve an tew—rive and toil; Thoddy— third horseman (the most junior); gainest—nearest; hoos— house; pikes—haystacks; boon—bound; jonny—jaunt; wer— our; lig leet—lie lightly.

A feature all three Ridings have in common is a brand of humour peculiar only to Yorkshire. A Yorkshireman's full-blooded humour is often in contrast with the more dour characteristics and brashness he has become noted for outside the county. His humour in the 19th century West Riding, as we have seen, frequently made tolerable the most depressing of living conditions in the towns. The late Arthur Jarratt in the latter part of the 20th century came to the fore as a dialect humorist and, just as John Hartley captured life in the textile belt in the telling of his tales and poems, so Arthur Jarratt gives us intimate glimpses of life in East Riding rural villages in the early years of the 20th century. His narrative poem, *Lang Sarmons*, is a good example of his ready wit and dry humour.

Lang Sarmons

Whenivver sarmon 's ower lang—an sum are to be sure—
It allus thinks me on aboot a spot called Botton Moor.
We ed a lahtle Bethil theer: it was a bonny place,
Ah offens used ti wend mi way ti seek oot Trawn o Grace.

An preeachers used ti cum tiv it, an mah wod, sum was queer!
Noo this consarns awd Peter Land; e'd cummed for monny a year.
E warn't si bad as preeachers go—is lungs were rare an sthrang!
Trouble with awd Peter was—e lasted ower lang!

Ah nivver took a deeal o nooat, a sooart o check ti keeap.
Ah nivver took mich nooatice cos Ah allus went ti sleeap.
Bud if ye rackoned up at all, Ah'll warrant ye'd be safe
If ye said is shortest sarman was an oor an a afe.

Noo, Ah leeaked efther chapil, an' steward, e was Ben:
An we ed oor stock ti fodder, we was nobbut labrin men.
An sooa, when Ben e sez ti me: "It's Peter Land next Sunda."
Sez Ah: "If summat isn't done, e'll ev us theer whahl Munda."

Sez Ben: "It's nobbut waste o tahm ti ax im ti be short,
We'll etti tak sum other rooad—noo, can ye think of aught?"
"Why ay," Ah sez. "Ah can an all; Ah sud a thowt afoor.
If Ah can onny work it, we'll be lowsed insahd an oor."

"Ah allus fills them chapil lamps ti top wi parafeen.
Next Sunda though, Ah deean't knaw as Ahs'll be si keen.
Ah'll mak it sooas them lamps'll fizzle oot at seven o'clock!
Ah rackon that'll give awd Peter Land a bonny shock!"

Sooa, when next Sunda cummed along, yon lamps was
                                         ommost dhry.
Ah's think the'd ardlins oil eneeaf ti dhroon a lahtle fly.
Ah sez ti Ben: "Ah onny ooaps we git collection taen."
"Well, if we deean't," sez Ben, "Ah rackon fooaks'll cum again."

Well, up cums Peter iv is thrap, an maks a goodish start;
An efther afe an oor we was well through fommost part.
So Ben teks up collection, an t'awd man puts on is specs,
An fun is place i Exodus, and fezzoned on is tex.

It was summat aboot Mawses— we'd eeard it oft afoor—
An' then Ah nooticed somehow light was lewking middlin poor.
Ah leeaned across ti Ben, an sez, when Peter starts ti spoot:
"Ah wunder wheer'll be Mawses when these chapil lights gan oot?"

It wasn't lang afoor fooaks was wunderin what was matter,
An t'poor awd man, e'd scarcelins getten Mawses oot o watter,
When yan o' t'lamps starts fickin, an it varry seean gans oot.
Ah'd been a thrifile ower keen i thrimmin that, Ah doot.

There was afe a dozen lamps i t'spot, an fost yan, then another
Went blobbin oot, an fooaks began ti get intiv a smother;
Till nobbut yan was left alight, an it nigh pulpit rail.
Thinks Ah: "It weean't be lang noo afoor it begins ti fail."

An Peter kep on preeachin—e nooaticed nowt was wrang:
E was reeadin frey is paper, an it kep im ower trang...
Bud that pulpit lamp kep bonnin as though it'd last all neet.
Ah deean't recall Ah've ivver knawn a lamp that bonnt si breet!

It'd brek mi eart ti tell ye ivvrything that we'd ti bahd.
An that dhratted lamp was bonnin efther fooaks'd got ootsahd.
We'd nivver been si late afoor—just wantin afe past nahn!
Sez Ben: "Thoo gits thi oil frey a better spot than mahn!"

At supper tahm, ma missus sez: "Yon lamps was rare 'n dhry!
Ah appened leeak at pulpit, so Ah filled it varry night"...
An next day, Ben, e sez ti me: "We'll thrim them lamps ni moor.
We'll etti just put clock on, like we've allus done afoor!"

sarman—sermon; ower lang—too long; It allus thinks me on —it always reminds me of; lahtle Bethil—little Bethel Non- conformist chapel; Trawn o Grace—Throne of Grace; sthrang—strong, oor an a afe—hour and a half; stock to fodder—cows to feed; wahl—until; lowsed—flnished and closed; ommost—almost; ardlins—scarcely; thrap—trap, car- riage; fommost—foremost; Mawses—Moses; middlin— rat her; gan oot—go out; fost yan—first one; ower trang— very busy.

End of century West Riding dialect writers are well represented in *An Anthology of West Riding Dialect Verse*, edited by Gwen Wade in 1964, but it by no means exhausts the number of people writing dialect in the West Riding. Indeed, since 1964 several new promising dialect-writers from this Riding have had verse published in the Y.D.S. annual publications, which have grown over the years.

One encouraging feature about West Riding dialect literature is the number of young authors trying their hands at it. Dr Ian Dewhirst, of Keighley, was still in his twenties when the West Riding Anthology was published, yet he was an established writer then and has continued to write as a local historian in Yorkshire. His poems reveal another characteristic of West Riding dialect that Bill Cowley commented upon—its capacity for adapting to modern idiom. In the present century it has changed considerably more than the dialects of the other two Ridings, and though it has lost a considerable number of long-established words from its vocabulary, it seems to be adding new ones from a variety of sources. Dialect is still widely used in the West Riding, even though it differs from the dialect spoken 50 or 60 years ago.

Warkin in t'Autumn by Ian Dewhirst

Warkin in t'autumn, wi t'owd leeaves come dahn
An caught in t'hedge lahk bits o' yeller rags,
An nowt but's wet, an t'earth all black and brahn,
An even t'flags
Slippy wi leeaves, an nivver dry all day:
Warkin in t'autumn, when there's not much leet,
Trailin abaht t'place, an t'paths slopped away,
Trod aht lahk girt soft cah-claps under t'feet.

Warkin in t'autumn, lapped i mist at nooin,
An t'trees at t'end o' t'run soa grey an bowed,
Wi t'murk a-drippin, suckin lahk a tune,
An t'beck soa loud,
An t'friendly hills gone, leeavin me aloan:
Warkin in t'autumn, luggin stuff abaht,
Fratchy wi t'face-itch, an damp through to t'boan,
All-ower muck, wearin t'owd jacket aht.

Warkin in t'autumn, clearin off t'deead things,
An puttin t'tools away till t'next tahm rahnd,
An all t'wahl there's a perky robin sings,
An wean't be drahned,
In t'empty elder-bush bi t'barrer-shed:
Warkin in t'autumn, ivvry tahm Ah pass,
Ah watch aht, grinnin, for his scrap o' red,
An whistle back at him across t'wet grass.

nowt but's wet—all is wet; cah-claps—cow dung; nooin— noon; lahk—like; beck—stream; fratchy—crotchety; boan—bone; next tahm rahnd—spring; barrer-shed—tool-shed.

Dr Dewhirst's wide range of nature dialect verse is well illustrated by the following poems, too, in contemporary dialect.

To snawdrops comin' too sooin.

Hah doesta time it ivvery year
I' t'deead o' Febrery?
One patch o' sun an' tha art here,
Snawdrops, soa bonnily,
To mak me feel spring mun be near
Through t'watched-for seet o' thee.

But, after all, tha's timed it wrong:
T'sun goes away, t'wind shifts,
It blaws a blizzard all neet long
An' buries thee i drifts,
An' th' art a draggled little throng,
Snawdrops, when t'frost lifts.

An' yet Ah bet if Ah could say,
"What art tha laikin' at?
Tha'st come too sooin bi monny a day,
An' getten pushed nigh flat,"
Tha'd pluck up cheek to answer, "Nay,
It's t'snaw 'at cam too lat!"

To a Moth

Tha'st t'whole wide neet to flitter through,
All sweet wi' t'scent o' leeaves an' dew,
An' yet it seeams my bit o' leet
Has ta'en thi fancy, tinsel-breet,
So tha mun bang wi' might an' main
Agen my cawd hard winderpane.

Ther's nowt mich here, for all it gleeams,
Just me sat wi' mi books an' dreeams;
Then wilta bruise thi dainty wings
Wi' strivin' after hoapless things,
When tha's got t'mooin and t'stars aht theear,
Saft petals fallin' far an' near?

An' yet ther's men, wi' t'warld to rooam,
Beat aht ther eager lives at hooam,

Each warmed wi' his awn can'el-flame
(An'whose to scorn, an' whose to blame?):
A call, a task, a lovin' face,
A vision, or a bidin'-place.

Thump on, then, though tha cannot pass,
Grey little ghoast agen the glass:
We've mich i' common, us an' thee,
Aw wodn't alter what mun be,
An, though tha haunt mi here all neet,
Wean't open t'latch, or put aht t'leet.

The late Fred Brown was a delightful man with a sense of dry humour quite his own. He was largely self-taught and worked all his life in the mill, but he penned some of the finest dialect verse of the 20th century, writing poems to suit most occasions and one of his poems had a very topical flavour in the 1960s, when the first men landed on the moon. His whimsical humour, half-satirical, half-serious, comes out strongly in *Hey Diddle Diddle*.

Hey diddle-diddle,
Three men on a griddle,
A rocket's landed on t'mooin;
A little germ laughed
To see such fun -
Ther'll be bother up theer varry sooin.

His more serious verse often underlines universal contemporary moral problems. A famous poem of his, *Gi' us Peace*, is a protest against war, its uselessness, horror and the misery it inflicts on the innocent. Fred Brown skilfully introduces pathos through the allegory of nature: the trees, the wind and a stream, who ask each other a hollow question, "Has man achieved universal peace yet?"

"Gi Us Peace" by Fred Brown

"Is it neya?" whispered t'trees;
"Maybe neya!" murmur'd t'wind;
"Happen neya!" burbl'd t'stream:
An t'trees—
An t'wind—
An t'stream
(In a queer waknin dream)
Ga voice to ther thowts
In t'whisperin.

"Ah'll goa!" said t'wind;
"Aye, goa!" urged t'stream;
"Do goa!" begged t'trees:
An t'quick wind went speedin
Wheer bairnies ligged bleedin,
Mangled an riven,
Stark-limbed,
God-given,
Tip-tossed childer.

Then follered wheer t'blast-guns,
Deeath's laikins, hed been;
An wistfully skenned
I' warrin men's een.

"Not yet!" grooaned t'trees
Foldin deep into t'neet;
"Not yet!" purled t'streeam
As it rullied fra t'seet.

neya—now; happen—perhaps; thowts—thoughts; bairnies— tiny children; ligged—lay; riven—torn apart; stark-lim bed— naked;

tip-tossed childer—-children thrown to one side; blast- guns—artillery; deeath's laikins—death's playthings; skenned —scanned; een—eyes; rullied—tumbled; fra t 'seet—from sight.

Gordon Allen North was another West Riding dialect-writer well known at the end of the 20th century as a contributor to Yorkshire periodicals and newspapers. Some of his most sensitive poems are love-poems. The three short love-poems by him below reveal the effectiveness of dialect verse in expressing love, as well as the humorous and tragic themes earlier.

"Nobbut a Leet"

Nobbut a leet
Winkin in t'neet
Upon th'heigh moor;

Nobbut a cry
Soft as a sigh
At a hawf-oppen door;

Nobbut a lad
Callin a glad
Greetin in t'dark;

Nobbut a lass
Hark'nin him pass,
Love in her heart.

heigh—high; hawf-oppen—half open.

"A Lovely Lass is Shoo"

Ah took her i mi airms today,
    A lovely lass is shoo;
Ah kussed her, an shoo bad me stay
    An stroke her achin broo;
Her skin's as snod as glass itsen,
    Her lips are honey-sweet:
Oh, what new wo'lds 'll oppen when
    Shoo's i mi airms toneet?

airms—arms; shoo—she; kussed—kissed; snod—smooth

"Love Song"

Keep thi lips for love, lass,
    An keep thi lips for me;
Share, if tha mun, thi beauty,
    An t'twinkle i thi ee,
An don thisen i' fol-de-rols
    For all the wo'ld to see—
But keep thi lips for love, lass,
    Oh keep thi lips for me.

mun—must; i' fol-de-rols—in fine clothes.

And finally a wedding blessing I was asked to compose for a young couple getting married in Yorkshire the year this edition came out, 2002:

Wedding Blessing in Yorkshire Dialect
by John Waddington-Feather

Soa, nah tha'rt wed an' made thi marriage vows,
an' ta'en each other better or for war,
we'll wish thee ivvery happiness an' joy
wherivver fortun taks thee, near or far.

Tha'rt sure to hev thi reg'lar ups-an'-dahns,
to fratch a bit an' sometimes shed a tear,
but nah tha'rt wed tha'll hev to mak it up
an' ho'd each other closer an' more dear.

Tha'll hev a deal o' happy times an' all,
but larn to share 'em wi' each other, too;
for sharing is what wedding's all abaht,
tha'rt joined as one i' wedlock nah, net two.

Soa, 'ere's a blessing on thi booath today,
a blessing on thi hooam an' on thi kin;
may God be wi' thee all thi wedded life,
enrich thee by His grace an' love. Amen.

fratch - quarrel

These, then, are just a few random selections from the works of Yorkshire dialect writers. It is difficult to say why writing in the dialect—in the north country dialects at any rate—continues to flourish to the extent it does. Membership of the Y.D.S. and interest in all kinds of matter connected with Yorkshire dialects have grown appreciably over the past few decades. A wide variety of factors influence Yorkshire men and women, some of them expatriates, to write in their local dialect.

One obvious reason is nostalgia for the past, a yearning for things associated with childhood and more idyllic days. But another important factor is the capacity Yorkshire dialect still has, in spite of limitations in vocabulary, to express vividly and simply matters that writers want to put down in a language that is part of their local heritage. It is a heritage started by Caedmon around the end of the seventh century and still continued by Yorkshire dialect-writers today.

For Further Reading

Parts One and Two: The Yorkshire Dialect Society's publications. The Y.D.S. now has a very full list of publications available and is constantly adding to it. This list is available if a s.a.e. is sent to the Hon. Librarian, The Y.D.S., Catherine Sowden, School of English, The University, Leeds LS2 9JT. Also published annually by the Y.D.S. are *Transactions* and *Summer Bulletin* which are sent free to members of the society.

Part One:

The Oxford Dictionary of Place-Names, E. Ekwall (Oxford 1960).

Survey of English Dialects, H. Orton et alia (Arnold, Leeds 1962-71).

A Word Geography of England, H. Orton and N. Wright (Seminar Press 1974).

Our Language, Simeon Potter (Penguin 1961). The volumes on Yorkshire place-names edited by A. H. Smith for the English Place-Name Society (Cambridge).

The English Dialect Dictionary, Joseph Wright (Oxford 1898-1905).

Lancashire Dialect, Peter Wright (Dalesman 1976).

English Dialects, M. F. Wakelin (Athlone Press 1977).

Discovering English Dialects, M. F. Wakelin (Shire Publications 1978).

Anglo-Saxon Christianity, Paul Cavill (HarperCollins, London 1999)
Basic Broad Yorkshire by Arnold Kellett. Available from the YDS

Part Two:

The WhiteRose Garland, W. J. Halliday and A. S. Umpleby (Dent 1949).

The York Cycle of Mystery Plays, J. S. Purvis (S.P.C.K. 1957).

The Wakefield Mystery Plays, M. Rose (Evans 1961).

The publications list of the Yorkshire Dialect Society.

Other works by John Waddington-Feather include:

CHILDREN'S NOVELS

The Quill Hedgehog novels are a series of children's environmental novels with animal characters. The first, Quill's Adventures in the Great Beyond, was written in the 1960s as a protest against pollution and urbanisation of the countryside.

The third Quill Hedgehog novel, Quill's Adventures in Grozzieland, was nominated for the Carnegie Medal. The first three novels have gone into three editions. A worthwhile read for children and adults alike

A1. Quill's Adventures in the Great Beyond. 87 pages. Paperback. Illustrated £5.99 $12 US. ISBN: 184175 180 4

A2. Quill's Adventures in Wasteland. 121 pages. Paperback. Illustrated £5.99 $12 US. ISBN:184175 181 2

A3. Quill's Adventures in Grozzieland. 116 pages. Paperback Illustrated £5.99 $12 US. ISBN:184175 182 0

A4. Quill's Adventures in Mereful. 88 pages Paperback. £5.99 $12 US. ISBN: 1 4137 1632 6

A5. Quill's Adventures in Humanfolkland. 97 pages. £5.99 $12 US ISBN: 1 84175 209 6

A6. Legends of Americada. 216 pp. An allegory in the Tolkien/Lewis tradition Paperback. £6.99 $15 US ISBN:1 84175 113 8

A7 Legends of Americada (part 2) unpublished.

A8. Legend Land. 134 pp. A children's fantasy novel. Paperback £5.99 $10 US ISBN: 1 84175 177 4

A.9 Legend Land (part 2) sequel to part 1. Unpublished

CRIME NOVELS

The Revd Detective Inspector Blake Hartley novels are set in the spectacular Yorkshire Pennine country. The lead character is an Anglican Non-Stipendiary priest, who with his loyal Muslim sergeant, Ibrahim Khan, solves crime on their home patch of Keighworth, West Yorkshire, and at times throughout the world.

B1. The Bradshaw Mystery. 176 pages. Paperback. £5.99 $12 US ISBN: 184175 044 1

B2. The Museum Mystery. 205 pages. Paperback. £5.99 ISBN: 1 84175 008 5

B3 The Marcham Mystery. 136 pages paperback £5.99 ISBN: 1 84175 094 8

B4. The Graveyard Mystery 160 pages paperback £5.99 ISBN: 1 84175 202 9

B5. The Allotment Mystery 134pp paperback. £5.99. ISBN: 1 84175 246 0.

B6 The Moorland Mystery Unpublished.

ROMANTIC HISTORICAL NOVELS

The 'Chance-Child' novels are a trilogy of romantic historical novels set among the wild Pennine Hills of West Yorkshire, Keighworth the mill town and locations abroad when members of the rival families find themselves involved in two World Wars and after. They are a saga of unremitting love and hate, tracing events of three generations united by blood but divided by class.

R1. Illingworth House The first in the Chance Child trilogy beginning in 1910 and covering events to 1930, setting the stage for the two sequels which follow. Paperback. 160pp £6.99 $17 US ISBN: 1 84175 212 6
North American edition ISBN 978 189731 236 9. $!7 US from Spire Publishing, Toronto.

R2. Chance Child (part 1) A romantic historical novel set in the West Riding and Prague between 1930 and 1945, covering events leading to the outbreak of war and the war itself. The novel contains strong emotional
content and portrays a violent battle between members of the English class system, as well as their war against the Nazis. 268 pp. Paperback £6.99 $15 US. ISBN 1 84175 130 8

R3. Chance Child (part 2)   covering events from 1945-60 Paperback. 188 pp £6.99 $15 US ISBN: 1 84175 142 1

DRAMA

C1. Garlic Lane.   27 pages. Paperback.   £5 $10 US
ISBN: 0 947718 64 8
A one-act humorous verse-play play set in West Yorkshire in the 1950s. First produced at Leeds Civic Theatre in 1972, it was revised and given a rehearsed reading by Bingley Little Theatre in 1998. In 1999 it was awarded the Burton Prize and described by one critic as the best verse-play since Under Milk Wood. A recording of the play was made live at Bingley Little Theatre in 1998 and is available on CD at £12 and cassette at £5. Its

London premiere was to a packed house at the Rosemary Branch Theatre in January 2010.

C2. Easy Street. 92 pages. Paperback. £3.50 $8 US ISBN: 1 84175 033 6
A humorous full-length verse-play set over a week (a day for each Sin) in a West Yorkshire mill town, with the Seven Deadly Sins acting as Narrators introducing each day's action. First produced at Leeds Civic Theatre in the 1970s and subsequently revised. Very suitable for book-in-hand readings or full stage production. An Introduction to the play by the scholar-poet Professor Walter Nash offers a penetrating critique of the play and the medieval Morality Play on which it is based.

C3 The Lollipop Man. A full-length play about the homeless – and much else – based on the author's experiences as chaplain in a Night Shelter and Prison. ISBN: 1 84175 132 4. £4.50

C4. Jonah A short play or musical suitable for school or church. Lasts about one hour as a play longer if produced a s short musical. Suitable for 10 to 14 year-olds.
ISBN: 1 84175 244 4 £.2.50.

C5. Behind Corridors of Power. A full-length play satirising politics and current political figures. The play also looks at life from the perspective of a high-ranking politician's wife whose husband unknown to her has a series of affairs, one with his diary secretary, whilst at Westminster. It also stresses the values of family life. ISBN: 1 84175 245 2. £4.50

C6. Tyndale. A full length play tracing the life and martyrdom of William Tyndale, the first translator of the Bible into English. A drama about free speech and religious freedom; set at a time when modern English evolved to become the global language of Shakespeare and his fellow writers a generation later. The play also covers events which marked the beginning of the Anglican Church. ISBN: 978 1 84175 223 5. £5.99

C7. Bill Braithwaite's Miracle. A full-length comedy about a family of self-made rich cousins who refuse to take in the black sheep of the family returning from Australia after 30 years, a dying impoverished man, as they imagine. When they discover he's a multi-millionaire they fall over themselves to accommodate him believing they're going to inherit his fortune as next of kin. He agrees to take up their offers – but imposes conditions; and therein lies the comedy.
ISBN: 978 1 84175 266 2. £4.50.

C8. The Secret Martyrs Against Hitler. A full-length play based on an account of the resistance against Hitler during the 1930s and 1940s inside Germany, culminating with Stauffenberg's bomb plot of 1944.
ISBN 978 1 84175 311 9. £5.99 $10 U.S..

C9. Limbo. A one and half hour play. Six souls from very different backgrounds find themselves waiting to be assessed for their next life. "Limbo" touches on religious themes, lightened, I hope, by comic touches and some commentary on contemporary events..ISBN:978 1 84175 308 9. £5,99 $10 U.S

C10. Bus-stop A one-act surrealistic play. Four characters, a young couple and an older couple. One set. Touches on contemporary issues. Plenty of humour. A surrealist play with audience rapport.
ISBN: 978 1 84175 309 6 £5 $10 U.S..

C11. Edward A full-length play about King Edward VIII and Mrs Simpson and the abdication crisis of 1936.
ISBN: 978 1 84175 314 0. £5.99 $10 US

VARIOUS

D3. Visions in the Winter Dark (Translations of three early Anglo-Saxon Christian poems with an Introduction for newcomers to A.-S. verse by Walter Nash). 32 pages Paperback. £5. $10 US ISBN: 1 84175 072 7

Y1. Yorkshire Dialect: a new comprehensive survey of the origins of English dialects and a selection of Yorkshire dialect literature from the 8th century poet Caedmon to the present. 100 pages. Paperback £6.99 ISBN: 1 84175 072 7

Y2. The Best of John Hartley An account of the life of the 19th century prolific Yorkshire Dialect writer, with selections from his work. A comprehensive vocabulary explains the dialect words used.
ISBN: 978 0 9556454 0 2. Paperback.107 pp. £6.99. $15 U.S.

S1. Ira and the Cycling Club Lion and other Short Stories A collection of short stories set in West Yorkshire and also Ukraine. Witty, droll, sad and some of them very amusing. Many were first published, after being translated into Russian, in the Ukrainian journal, 'Porto Franko. They are now gaining popularity in other parts of Europe. 120 pages. Paperback. £6.99 $15 U.S. ISBN: 1 84175 240 1.

S2. Feather's Miscellany 1 2007 . An annual publication from Feather books comprising a collection of short stories, poetry,

extracts from his drama and novels, essays and anecdotes by Revd John Waddington-Feather. Suitable for recital, staged and rehearsed readings, quotations and articles for magazines.
ISBN: 978 1 84175 279 2   110 pp   £7.99 $17 US

S3. Feather's Miscellany 2 2008 . An annual publication from Feather books comprising a collection of short stories, poetry, essays and anecdotes by Revd John Waddington-Feather. Suitable for recital, rehearsed readings, quotations and articles for magazines.
ISBN: 978 1 84175 279 2   110 pp   £9.99 $20 US

S4. Feather's Miscellany 3 2009 . An annual publication from Feather books comprising a collection of short stories, poetry, essays and anecdotes by Revd John Waddington-Feather. Suitable for recital, rehearsed readings, quotations and articles for magazines.
ISBN: 978 1 84175 306 5.   190 pp   £9.99 $20 US

M6. Seasons and Occasions. (Book 1) A collection of 50 hymns and songs by David Grundy and John Waddington-Feather.   £6.99 $15 US.   ISBN: 1 84175 162 6

M7. Seasons and Occasions (Book 2) The third collection of 50 hymns and anthems by David Grundy and John Waddington-Feather.

M8. Hymns from the Classics A collection of 50 hymns the tunes of which are taken from Classical Music. Like the other collection of hymns these cover most of the Church's Calendar. £6.95 $14 US.   ISBN: 978 1 84175 213 4

M9. Judas A sequence of dramatic monologues and hymns

for Lent and Passiontide. Music by David Grundy. Premiered in 2009 by a leading Yorkshire choir and readers at Ilkley, Yorkshire. Words by John Waddington-Feather. A4 £6.99 $15 US ISBN 978 1 84175 302 7S

M10. Isaiah A sequence of dramatic monologues and hymns for Advent and Christmas. Music by David Grundy. Words by John Waddington-Feather. £6.99 $15 US ISBN 978 1 84175 307 2

M11. Magdalene A sequence of dramatic monologues and hymns for Easter. Music by David Grundy. Words by John Waddington-Feather . To be published in 2010

M12. Matthias A sequence of dramatic monologues and hymns for Pentecost/Trintiy. Music by David Grundy, Words by John Waddington-Feather. ISBN: 978 1 84175 313 3 £6.99 $15 U.S. ISBN 978-1-84175-302-7 U.K. £ 6.95

G1. Pilgrimages. An anthology of poetry to commemorate the tenth anniversary of The Poetry Church magazine, the Christian poetry quarterly published by Feather Books. Edited by Professor Walter Nash, this is a milestone in Christian poetry publishing. £13.99 $28 US. ISBN 1 84175 224 X